THE
GREAT WESTERN
RAILWAY
IN THE
1930s

Volume Two

ISBN 1-870754-40-9
Printed by: Amadeus Press Ltd., Huddersfield
First Published 1987, reprinted 1997

THE
GREAT WESTERN
RAILWAY
IN THE
1930s

Volume Two

Compiled by
David Geen ● Barry Scott

From the collection of
Mr. G.H. Soole

Runpast Publishing
10 Kingscote Grove, Cheltenham, Glos, GL51 6JX

Biography

Godfrey Hewitt Soole was born in the Derbyshire village of Creswell, the son of the local vicar. His father was reappointed to another parish, in Huddersfield, where Bill, as he was known, was brought up. He attended the Grammar School and went to Cambridge in 1931, at about the time his father became vicar to Emmanual Church in Clifton, Bristol. So began G.H. Soole's association with this famous old city.

In 1938, G.H. Soole joined the Great Western Railway as a traffic apprentice. Apparently this involved him travelling to other stations to 'learn his trade', so giving him ample opportunity to pursue his hobby, the results of which we see in this book and in Volume I. It is said that the GWR frowned upon its employees taking photographs and that he was discouraged, so during 1938 his hobby gradually ceased.

Called up at the outbreak of the Second World War, Bill served in the Royal Engineers, rising to the rank of Major in charge of No. 181 R.O.C. This took him to India and Europe, with service in Germany after the war until his demob in 1946 when he returned to the Great Western.

His subsequent work took him away from Bristol until 1952, when he returned to take up a permanent position, rising to become Assistant Divisional Superintendent. In 1970, he died suddenly at the age of 57. His widow, Mrs. M. Soole, gave his collection to the National Railway Museum, where it is held in trust for the nation.

Introduction

Since the first volume was published in 1985, many people have written asking when this second book would be ready. We have had much pleasure in compiling it and hope the reader enjoys it also!

In Volume II we have tried to provide more in-depth information, some of which was not available to us in 1982 when we compiled the first book, to give the railway enthusiast, modeller, or casual reader, a better insight into the Great Western Railway of the 1930s.

Those intervening years have also enabled us to look more closely into the background of the period. The earlier photographs were taken in a climate of depression and high unemployment whilst the later views, as one of the captions relates, were photographed during a period of international tension and gathering war clouds, culminating in 1939 with the beginning of the Second World War. Through the lens of Mr. Soole's camera, we have a unique collection of photographs, taken largely within a twenty mile radius of the centre of Bristol, capturing the changing face of a single railway through a time span of some five years. Against the political, international and economic backcloth it is possible to see the character of the railway changing as it competes for freight traffic and passengers, not only from other railways but from the increasing volume of road transportation. The Great Western can be seen introducing new locomotives and carriages, modernising stations and improving routes and facilities, in an effort to stay competitive. Perhaps this is the finest collection of photographs taken showing a railway during such a short, but fascinating and important time in our recent history.

Further efforts have been made by more detailed study and prolonged research to establish a pattern of dates and events. In this we have been successful, due sometimes, let us add, to information supplied to us by others, to whom we shall be forever grateful. Other odd snippets of information have been gleaned from some notes Mr. Soole wrote on the reverse of photographs he supplied to friends, which were not written into the notes of his photographic catalogue. We have endeavoured to include all of this in this second volume.

In order to maintain the theme and link the books so that they might be read together, we have numbered this work consecutively with the first volume. This aids reference to earlier photographs by not having two similar numbers.

We hope you enjoy this second volume and we would like to record our thanks to those people who kindly wrote to us, providing the inspiration.

Just as this book was being prepared for publication, an important document was loaned to the NRM. This, in Mr. Sooles writing, must have formed a record of his photographic collection. Although this document only covered the first year or so of his work, we have included all the information applicable to this and the earlier volume. We trust that the delay has been worthwhile.

That uniquely numbered 'Castle' No. 100 A1 *Lloyds* leaves Temple Meads station. Originally built in 1907 as No. 4009 *Shooting Star*, it was withdrawn in 1925 only to reappear shortly afterwards rebuilt as a 'Castle'. It retained its old name and number until January 1936 when it was ceremoniously altered to 'A1' *Lloyds* the number '100' being added the following month. The two cast plates can be seen on the cab side, as can the odd layout of the numbers on the front buffer-beam. This was the first 'Castle' withdrawn (1950) at which time there were ten 'Castles' still to be built – but by then this locomotive was over forty years old and had run almost two million miles. A small plate was added beneath the nameplate in July 1939, proclaiming 'Castle Class'. The train is a mixture of designs and styles and varying waist levels. Leading is a family saloon originally of diagram G33 but because the guards projections have been removed it has become diagram G45. These were built around 1900 and could be used as invalid saloons by having a couch suspended on slings from the ceiling. Those were later replaced by side settees and became just for family use. This would of course include servants and a small galley was provided for them to carry out their duties. A number of these vehicles were used as ward cars and officers accommodation in World War I. The brake third behind this is a very new diagram D124, only introduced that year (1937). The stock gets older towards the back and bringing up the rear are a LNER perishable van and a G.W. horsebox.

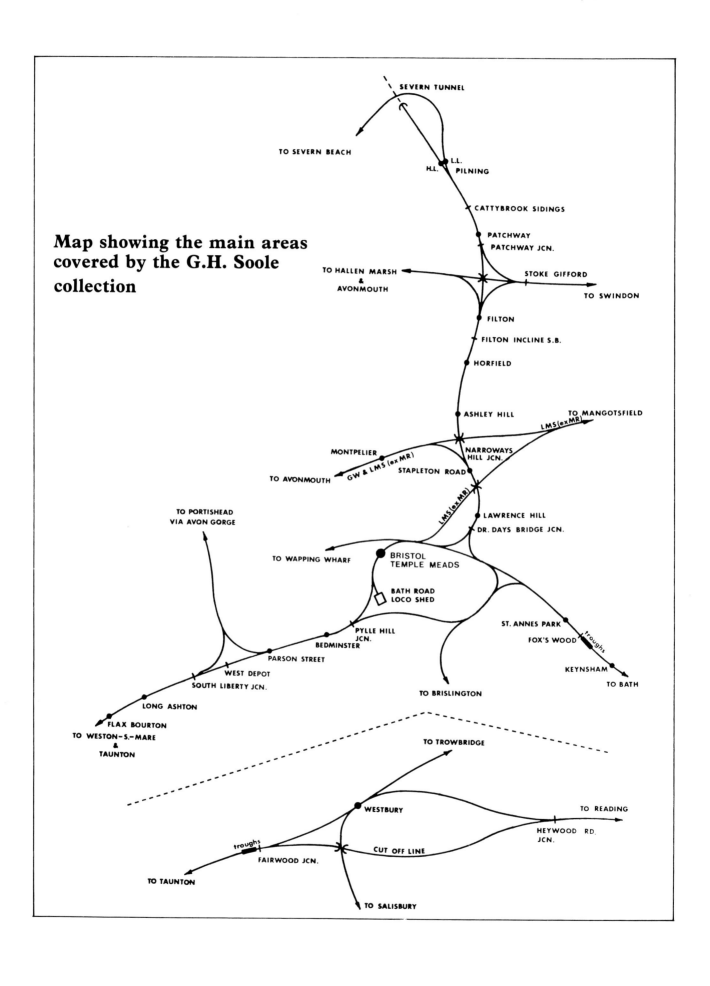

Map showing the main areas covered by the G.H. Soole collection

SEVERN TUNNEL

TO SEVERN BEACH

H.L. L.L. PILNING

CATTYBROOK SIDINGS

PATCHWAY
PATCHWAY JCN.

TO HALLEN MARSH & AVONMOUTH

STOKE GIFFORD

TO SWINDON

FILTON

FILTON INCLINE S.B.

HORFIELD

ASHLEY HILL

TO MANGOTSFIELD

LMS (ex MR)

MONTPELIER

NARROWAYS HILL JCN.

GW & LMS (ex MR)

STAPLETON ROAD

TO AVONMOUTH

LMS (ex MR)

TO PORTISHEAD VIA AVON GORGE

LAWRENCE HILL

DR. DAYS BRIDGE JCN.

TO WAPPING WHARF

BRISTOL TEMPLE MEADS

BATH ROAD LOCO SHED

ST. ANNES PARK

FOX'S WOOD

troughs

PYLLE HILL JCN.

BEDMINSTER

PARSON STREET

KEYNSHAM

TO BATH

WEST DEPOT

SOUTH LIBERTY JCN.

TO BRISLINGTON

LONG ASHTON

FLAX BOURTON

TO WESTON-S.-MARE & TAUNTON

TO TROWBRIDGE

WESTBURY

TO READING

HEYWOOD RD. JCN.

troughs

CUT OFF LINE

FAIRWOOD JCN.

TO TAUNTON

TO SALISBURY

135. A 'down' local train makes its way along the slow line near Twyford. This section of line has two pairs of 'up' and 'down' tracks, as today. To the right of the engine the pointwork leads to a refuge, laid between these two sets. The signals on the left are set over at the wrong side, probably to aid sighting because the bridges behind would hinder a clear view. Swindon-based No. 2938 *Corsham Court*, a member of the famous 'Saint' class, heads west. Built in 1911 it was soon to be fitted with outside steam pipes, in February 1935. It also still retains the upper lamp bracket above the smokebox rather than on the door itself. Beneath the buffer beam is the ATC shoe. Behind the tender, one of the 3,500 gallon variants, this one by Collett, are two 70′ dining cars, hardly local stock. The first is one of the massive Dreadnoughts of 1904, diagram H8-11 with an H24 next. These were easily recognisable with their flat sides, making an interesting comparison in styles.

136. 'Bulldog' 4-4-0 No. 3407 *Madras* reaches the summit at Patchway with an 'up' express during the winter of 1934-35. This engine was shedded at Severn Tunnel Junction at this time so it may be deputising for a failed engine. An 8-week spell in the workshops at Newport during 1934 is still apparent as the engine is in a nice condition. 'Bulldogs' were allocated to Severn Tunnel Junction for pilot duties, as elsewhere. Until December 1933, No. 3407 had been fitted with Westinghouse brake equipment, used when running with stock from other companies, principally those from the LNER. However, by the late 1920s most of the previously fitted air-braked stock had either been replaced or converted to vacuum braking, thus making the equipment redundant. On the side of the smokebox, barely visible just above the saddle, is a patch covering the hole through which passed the exhaust pipe from the Westinghouse pump. Behind the tender is one of the GW prize cattle wagons or 'Beetles' as they were called. The train is a Cardiff – Bristol one. The short signal to the left is soon to be replaced with a taller version and the 3′ shunting arm replaced with a smaller arm.

139. An unidentified '63XX' passes over the water troughs at Fox's Wood with an 'up' freight, heading towards Bath from Bristol. Behind the footbridge is the water tank which feeds the troughs. The water fed to this tank from the river Avon also supplied the main water tanks at both Bristol Bath Road and St. Philips engine sheds. The engine is rather grimy, certainly it has not been cleaned for some time. Of note is the ATC shoe at the front which has not much clearance between it and the water. The left-hand lamp has SPM stencilled on it meaning it is from St. Philips Marsh Shed. Note the sections of Barlow rail used as a drain cover. On the right is what looks like a walkway with short lengths of timber laid on the ballast at the sleeper ends.

Opposite page top:
137. A 'down' 'express' approaches Flax Bourton station in the summer of 1935, it could in fact be August Bank Holiday Monday. Although fitted with an express headcode the train is in fact an excursion from Bristol to Weston-Super-Mare. Many eager faces can be seen at the coach windows, no doubt anxious to reach their destination. Prior to the advent of private cars for the masses and the long distance motor coach, this was a familiar sight at holiday times, the railways providing the only viable means of transporting a large number of people over any distance. These excursion trains often provided the enthusiast with unusual locomotives and coaching stock as every available item was pressed into service. The engine, No. 2340 of the 'Dean Goods' type, was over fifty years old when photographed here and had eventually a total life of 70 years. Built in 1884, it was originally constructed with an S2 boiler with round topped firebox, the dome then being on the first ring of the boiler. The dome was moved to the second ring in 1901 and then in 1904 an S4 boiler was fitted with the dome in the position shown here. Finally, a Belpaire firebox replaced the round top type in 1913. A superheater and ATC apparatus were fitted in the early 'thirties. No. 2340 was withdrawn originally in June 1939 but reinstated in early 1940 owing to the demands of World War II on the railway system. When seen here the locomotive was based at St. Philips Marsh shed at Bristol, in earlier years it had been at Reading among other allocations.

Opposite page bottom:
138. A tank engine, with express headlamps, speeds along the relief lines near Goring with a 'down' train. It was often said of trains such as this one that they only had to miss out a couple of stations to be classed as expresses. This is probably an Oxford train and Mr. Soole was standing on the 'up' main when taking the photograph. No. 6105 was one of the first of the '61XX' class, completed in May 1931, and allocated to Slough. Designed to do the sort of task seen here, all 70 of these locomotives were in the London division, running accelerated services. When first built, No. 6105 did not have sliding shutters on the cab side but, as can be seen, these were soon fitted. The leading vehicle is a rather elderly Dean brake third, of diagram D21, which looks to have recently been repainted.

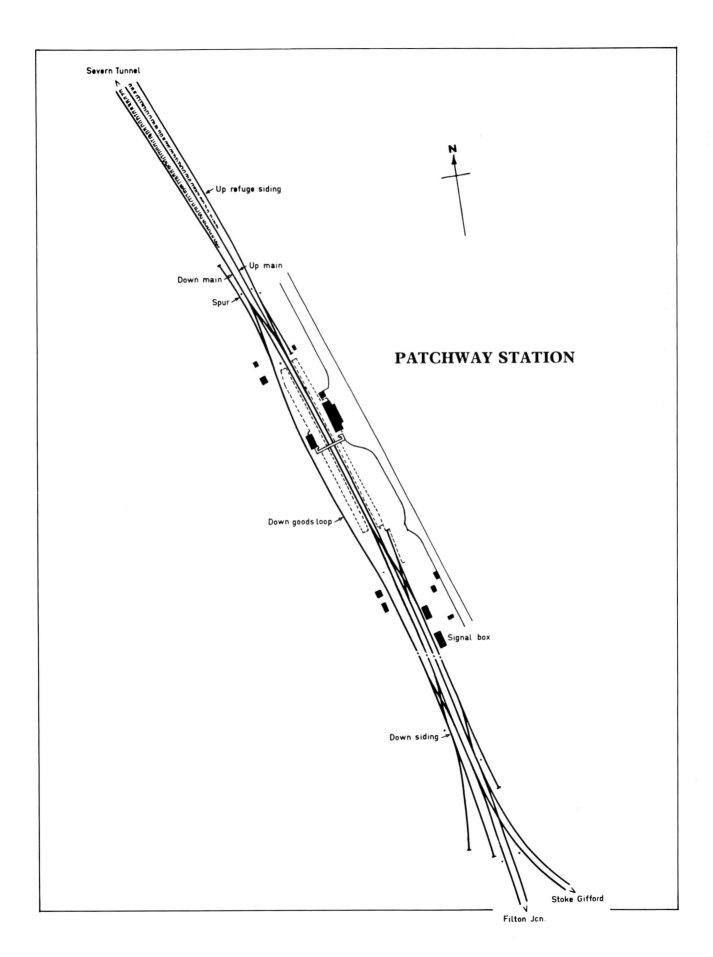

Severn Tunnel

Up refuge siding

N

Up main

Down main

Spur

PATCHWAY STATION

Down goods loop

Signal box

Down siding

Stoke Gifford

Filton Jcn.

140. Taken from outside Patchway Incline signalbox, the differing levels between the 'up' and 'down' lines is very apparent in the view. An 'up' freight climbs past the box, passing under the A38 roadbridge with the longer 'up' tunnel beyond, from which a banking engine has just emerged. To the left, on the upper level, can be seen a board telling drivers of freights to stop to allow the wagon brakes to be pinned down, the gradient, here 1 in 80, changes to 1 in 68 immediately past the 'down' tunnel. Alongside the track is a footpath, making it safe for guards working at night. This area was also the site of an earlier Patchway station, closed in August 1885. No. 5255 climbs steadily up the hill with its freight, consisting mostly of coal but with at least one van and a tank wagon included. Shedded at Aberdare, this '52XX' has not many weeks left before it is laid aside. Having recently had almost two months in the works at Swindon, it returned to service in early October but was taken to Caerphilly Stock Sheds on the 28th December. The following year it returned to Swindon and was rebuilt into one of the '72XX' 2-8-2T, and renumbered 7220. This was the first of this class to appear with a straight footplate, in September 1935. In 1940 Swindon was to build another 2-8-0T numbered 5255.

141. The coaching stock on this 'up' express bends over the summit into Patchway station after the long 8-mile climb from some 140' below the River Severn, on an average gradient of 1 in 100. No. 4073 *Caerphilly Castle* and her train are signalled to take the London line. No. 4073 is one of the most famous locomotives, being the first of the magnificent 'Castle' class. During 1934 this locomotive moved from its London shed, via Swindon Works, to Cardiff for seven months then on to Llandore. Note the 6-mile post on the right-hand platform. This gives the distance to Bristol, from where the original South Wales route leaves the main line at 'South Wales Junction'. Also to be seen are the number of signals including the ground pattern at this point, covering sidings, main lines, junctions, crossover and goods refuge (behind the train). The tall bracket signal above the train, soon to be replaced, indicates the train is eastbound towards London.

142. The 9.15 a.m. Paddington – Taunton express stands at Bristol Temple Meads station on a fine Tuesday in 1935. This train arrived shortly after midday and departed again for Taunton at 12.15 p.m. It is almost 12.10 p.m. so there is a little time in hand for the fireman to look around. The chap with the hammer on the platform is either a wheel-tapper or a ganger. The train engine No. 4056 *Princess Margaret* of Taunton shed is working home. Having had visits to both Swindon and Newton Abbot Works' the previous year, it is not surprising that the locomotive has had some minor changes. These include having a whistle shield fitted and the front lampbracket moved from the smokebox top to the door in addition to the short safety valve cover replacing the usual taller version. The tender is one of the twenty 4,000 gallon types designed by Dean and constructed between 1900 and 1904. This one, No. 1461, was the last tender of the first batch built in 1900. These tenders were mainly for general use, appearing behind many different locomotives and several classes, although a few were built to run with Churchward's prototypes. The vehicle behind the tender was once part of Queen Victoria's 1897 Royal Train, this being one of a pair of brake vans. When the GWR dispensed with its own Royal train in 1927 this vehicle and its sister went into service as special vans, going out on a regular schedule to the West of England. This particular van, No. 1069, supplied hotels and refreshment rooms owned by the Great Western with fresh linen, etc., each week. On Tuesday the van left Paddington on the 9.15 a.m. and was worked to Taunton, arriving at 2.0 p.m. At 3.40 p.m. it left again, this time to Plymouth. The following day it returned to Taunton on its way back to London. The train itself was also very interesting, normally leaving Paddington with up to 10 coaches, usually 9 plus the van. Two coaches were detached at Swindon for Cheltenham, then after Bristol 2 or 3 were again detached, including a refreshment car at Weston-Super-Mare, depending on which day it was[1]

143. Fresh from Swindon Works, a 'Star' runs into Pilning station with a lightweight Cardiff-Bristol express. No. 4055 *Princess Sophia* spent ten weeks going through the shops and was sent to Bath Road Shed for 1 week, then on again to Old Oak Common for four weeks before returning to Bristol. During its next visit to the Works in May 1935, the Churchward tender here was exchanged for the 'intermediate' type seen in plate 32 in Volume 1. This lasted only twelve months before the Collett 4,000 gallon version was added in June 1936. Built on the eve of the Great War, No. 4055 has had the upper lamp bracket moved to the smokebox door and apart from this and the removal of the splasher beading, is virtually as built. Its train is of Collett-built coaches although the second vehicle is one of the wide bodied 1929 Riviera stock, the extra width being clearly seen. The locomotive is crossing the 'up' refuge pointwork and from this photograph it is not apparent that it is climbing the gradient, being 1 in 100 all the way from the bottom level in the Severn Tunnel.

144. The 11.45 a.m. Bristol-Paddington, behind No. 4033 *Queen Victoria* of the 'Star' class, storms past the signalbox on Filton incline, hiding it in the exhaust. Built in 1910, the locomotive had only recently arrived at Bristol Bath Road shed from Worcester via Swindon works, and is still in excellent condition. It was to be a regular on this train. As well as a Collett 4,000 gallon tender, it has received a whistle shield and the upper lamp bracket moved to the smokebox door. The tender here was only used from May 1935 until January 1936, when a Churchward type, seen later, was substituted. Behind the locomotive is a mixture of coaching stock, the leading vehicle being a 1929 Riviera brake third of the maximum width as can be readily seen in comparison with the next coach. The centre three vehicles is one of the 1925 articulated diner sets, and to the rear a Concertina composite. The train is running on the new lines, opened in 1933, to Filton Junction where it will turn east to London. The photograph was taken from the adjacent footbridge.

145. The pride of the Great Western Railway's locomotive fleet, No. 6000 *King George V*, stands at the head of the 'down' Bristolian, this may have in fact been the inaugural run. Steam hides a lot of the front of this magnificent locomotive, including the famous bell presented to it by the Baltimore and Ohio Railway (and later stolen by some GI servicemen during World War II as were the badges on the cabside). So much has been written about this engine, which has been preserved and is still running, albeit in BR livery, that one could probably fill the book with facts and photographs. However, fittingly, we see it here in the GWR Centenary year.

146/147. Two photographs which show firstly, below, one of Bristol's allocation of big 2-6-2Ts standing at the east end of Temple Meads with an 'up' express, steam leaking from virtually every joint. It is difficult to judge what is happening. Mr. Soole records that this as an engine failure, but which one? In the second photograph – above – No. 5022 *Wigmore Castle* can be seen with the same train and is carrying a local code which was a regular occurrence for trains starting from Weston-Super-Mare working to Bristol as locals then proceeding as an express. Has another, third locomotive failed with No. 5158 bringing in the train for No. 5022 to take on, or has either Nos. 5158 or 5022 failed? Certainly, the tank engine looks unhealthy. At the front of the train can be seen Collett brake third No. 4943 of diagram D95 built in 1927 on Lot 1375.

148. A southerly wind throws the smoke from this 'up' express across the countryside as it approaches the station at Pilning, climbing away from the Severn Tunnel. The low wintry sun reflects from the insulators on the telegraph poles. This is a Cardiff – Paddington train hauled by No. 5004 *Llanstephan Castle* which has been fitted with a BTH speedometer, these becoming standard items by late 1935 when we see it here. Behind the tender, the leading coach is a 70′ third of diagram C38, a late steel panelled Toplight. Next follows one of a pair of converted brake thirds which were equipped with a small buffet and another 70′ vehicle, this a dining car of H13 diagram. During World War II new long refuge sidings were laid on either side of the main line as we see it here from Pilning to Ableton Lane Tunnel, in the distance through the second bridge. This was to allow trains to wait nearer the entrances and exits of the tunnel under the Severn, saving precious time between these sidings and allowing a greater number of trains to pass through.

149. 'Star' class No. 4061 *Glastonbury Abbey* climbs away from Ableton Lane Tunnel which was between the Severn Tunnel and Pilning station. The train is a Cardiff – Brighton, composed mainly of Southern Railway stock but with at least one GW coach at the rear. The Southern vehicles that are discernible are ex-LSWR 'Ironclads' with their rather curious bogies, called 'Dreadnoughts'. The Southern built a number of these coaches after the grouping but mostly with a different design of bogie. The GW coach may have been a 'strengthening' vehicle, added when necessary. All the major GW stations were allocated a number of 'spare' coaches in case a train was over-filled or a vehicle had to be removed for attention. Through the left arch of the overbridge can be seen a footbridge with the tunnel beyond. Above this in the far distance is the chimney for one of the Severn Tunnel pumping stations which pumped millions of gallons a day to prevent the tunnel from flooding. On the right the PW huts have a guard rail to prevent the workmen walking into the path of a train.

150. A north to west express comes over the summit into Patchway station, and is signalled to take the Bristol line at the junction ahead. Sent new to Shrewsbury shed when completed in May 1934, No. 5032 *Usk Castle*, looking in need of a clean, was a frequent performer on this train. It will be replaced at Bristol. The vehicle behind the engine is one of the cattle vans, code named 'Beetle', used for transporting prize animals to shows, etc. On the siding, waiting for the road with a 'down' goods train returning empty wagons to South Wales, is a member of the 'Star' class. Of particular interest is the lamp-post. The oil lamp itself is missing, removed at daylight by a porter. It will be replaced later, lit and winched up into the holder at dusk.

151. Leaking steam from its inside cylinders, a pristine member of the 'Star' class No. 4034 *Queen Adelaide* heads east with a Cardiff-Paddington express. The location is Stoke Gifford Junction. The sparkling condition of No. 4034 following a recent visit to the Works is apparent. It was while there in mid 1932 that it was fitted with elbow steam pipes – unfortunately hidden by steam here. It has had the lamp bracket fitted to the door and received a short safety valve cover. Behind the engine's 3,500 gallon tender is one of the 1929 Riviera brake thirds, which were to the widest possible gauge, followed by a contrasting 70′ slab-sided restaurant car. Members of a track gang watch Mr. Soole, whilst behind them, perched rather periously it would seem is a fogmans hut.

152. Rushing out of Patchway New Tunnel we see a north to west express, pulled by No. 5016 *Montgomery Castle* of Newton Abbot Shed. This tunnel was opened in 1887 and was exactly 1 mile long on a rising gradient of 1 in 100. Above, to the left, is the 'down' line which continued in a cutting before disappearing into the shorter, 1,250 yard long 'down' tunnel. This was the original single line to the New Passage pier (for steamers) opened in 1863 by the grand sounding 'Bristol and South Wales Union Railway' – all 11½ miles of it to Broad Gauge, which from the outset was worked by the GWR. This route was designed as a short cut to Cardiff and South Wales using steamers for the short journey across the Severn, rather than the much longer journey via Gloucester. With the opening of the Severn Tunnel under the river the route was altered at Pilning and eventually the pier closed.

Opposite page top:
153. The banking engine emerges from the one-mile long Patchway New Tunnel as it assists a heavily laden coal train to the summit. There, the banker and its tunnel van will drop off whilst the train then continues. The train engine is a South Wales allocated '28XX' class 2-8-0, No. 2821. It appeared in early 1907 as the first engine of the third batch and was built with a short-coned boiler and short smokebox and without top feed. The top feed was fitted to these engines very quickly after their introduction, Churchward recognising at once the savings in wear and corrosion and the fuel economies that this meant. In May 1909, No. 2821 received its first long-coned boiler, reverted to the earlier type nine months later but in September 1915 returned to a long-coned type for good. The ATC apparatus was fitted in the early 'thirties to the whole class. The ballast has been removed from the track on which this 'H' class goods is running. The new material has been dropped but the distribution and packing has yet to be finished. Straddling the cutting is the graceful brick road bridge which carries the main A38 road.

Opposite page bottom:
154. This engine, No. 4301, completed in June 1911, was the first of many 2-6-0s to be built. It was an example of one of the GW's most successful designs and the first locomotive to be fitted with top feed from new. It was also one of the last to be fitted with a brass Swindon Works plate. In fact this unique engine hadn't many months service left when photographed early in 1936 as it was withdrawn from St. Philips shed, Bristol, in the August. Its wheels and motion were re-used for a 'Grange' class locomotive, No. 6818 *Hardwick Grange*, completed in December of the same year. In this photograph No. 4301 is at the head of an 'up' 'H' class goods train climbing towards Patchway Tunnel and assisted by a '3150' class 2-6-2T banking engine. The photograph is taken from Cattybrook signalbox. On the left, a 'down' freight can be seen descending towards Pilning and the Severn Tunnel, the 'down' line falling away very quickly from the 'up' line. The gradients were 1 in 68 'down' and 1 in 100 'up' at this point. Of interest is the rather tight crossing into the sidings on the right, these giving access into the Cattybrook Brickworks.

155. No. 5007 *Rougemont Castle* climbs past Narroways Junction, under the LMS line and on up the hill out of the basin in which Bristol sits. Ahead is another two miles of mostly 1 in 75 climbing to Filton. This express is supposed to be the 5.15 p.m. Bristol – Paddington but earlier views show this train to have more modern stock available to it. The engine was around this time at Old Oak Common but transferred to Wolverhampton, so this in fact might be the 10.45 a.m. Penzance – Wolverhampton, the coach formation fitting this exactly. It would have passed through Bristol at about 5.15 p.m., possibly causing the incorrect identification. If so this train will run via Filton Junction and onto the LMS line and the former Bristol and Gloucester at Westerleigh Junction as far as Standish Junction where it will return to GW metals. No. 5007 has not had the fire-iron tunnel added yet over the rear splashers. When built in 1927 it was among the last with the old inside cylinder cover and to appear with the smaller 3,500 gallon tender. The leading coach is a Toplight brake third, No. 2379 to diagram D47 completed on Lot 1195 in November 1911, followed by another Toplight, this time a 70′ composite. The LMS line crossing over at this point was the link between the main line into Bristol from Mangotsfield and the joint GW/LMS to Clifton.

156. Under a stormy sky, the 5.15 p.m. Bristol-Paddington express approaches the junction at Filton station where it will turn east. This train is the return working of the 'down' 'Bristolian' arriving at Paddington at 6.30 p.m., ready for the following days 'down' trip again. The engine too is working home, back to Old Oak Common Shed. The centre vehicle of the set is a buffet car introduced in 1931 for short, quick journeys such as this. No. 6027 *King Richard I* was for most of her GW career based in London, before moving to Devon. In 1950, whilst working one of the portions of a 'down' Cornish Riviera Express, it was involved in a minor accident near Westbury, hitting a tractor on a crossing, one of its passengers that day being none other than Winston Churchill

159. No. 4068 *Llanthony Abbey* climbs the gradient towards Filton Incline signalbox with a 'down' north to west express and is just passing under the A38 road. This engine is one of Shrewsbury's allocation of 'Stars', ten or eleven being shedded there by the mid-thirties. It was one of the last of the class to be built, in fact in the same year as the first of the 'Castle' class. It is therefore not surprising that within a couple of years after this photograph, it was rebuilt as a 'Castle'. The leading vehicle behind the engine was originally a 48′ clerestory van built on the MR Lot 880 during 1914 and numbered 118. This was changed in 1933 by the LMS to No. 32828. The eliptical roof was fitted around 1919 and was to diagram D1067. Some of these vans were used for pigeon traffic, having tip-up shelves provided. The outward opening sliding doors are to be noted. Further down the train is another LMS coach, in this case a 12-wheel diner of diagram 1743.

Previous page top:
157. A Cardiff-Brighton express, composed of Southern Railway carriages, passes Filton Incline signalbox and its interesting junction signal as it climbs towards Patchway. At its head is No. 4045 *Prince John*. This was named after the youngest of King George V's five sons who died while still only a youth. This was the only member of the 'Star' class built after the 1911 batch to carry a short-coned boiler, this being fitted in 1915 and removed during 1917. The engine is known to have run coupled with the 8-wheel tender built for *The Great Bear* at about this time in the summer of 1936 but as we see here, it is equipped with a standard 3,500 gallon version. The front lamp bracket has been moved to the smokebox and a whistle shield added but other than this, it is in near original condition. The SR set No. 436 is an ex-LSWR set of Ironclad coaches. The Southern built some similar vehicles but these were not fitted with the distinctive Dreadnought bogies which those above have. The set comprises brake third No. 3189, first No. 7186, one third of either No. 721 or 722 with another brake third, No. 3188 being the last member of the set. Two Maunsell coaches bring up the rear. This was supposedly the last set fitted with these bogies. The roof destination boards seen on top of the third must only have been visible to signalmen in that position! The signal indicates that the train will take the Bristol route (stopping at Stapleton Road not Temple Meads) and that the junction at Patchway is clear. This is a splitting distant, the top home signal being common to both. Above the engine is the access gate and path from the station road down to the signalbox. A lovely photograph.

Previous page bottom:
158. The 11.55 a.m. Paddington-Swansea sweeps down the hill towards Patchway Long Tunnel. This train will divide, the last vehicle going to Pembroke Dock, the five behind the dining car to Milford Haven while the first four remain at Swansea. The train is mostly comprised of modern carriage stock with the exception of the large Dreadnought restaurant car. No. 4083 *Abbotsbury Castle* is from Cardiff shed and is still carrying the old pre 1934 insignia on its tender. The sun throws an interesting shadow onto the trackside, the pipe for the 4-cone ejector and handrail are clearly definable. This engine was the first in the second batch of 'Castles', built in 1925. Clearly visible on the front footplate is the 'joggle' set in the engines frames to permit clearance for the bogie swing. This was altered from No. 4093 onwards but was a feature of the first twenty 'Castles' and all of the 'Star' class. The 'down' line swings away from the 'up' line as can be observed, and enters the 1,260-yard long tunnel, emerging for a short distance and then passing through the 62-yard short tunnel, both opened as part of the Bristol and South Wales Union Railway in 1863 and originally broad gauge. With the opening of the Severn Tunnel, a new tunnel was dug to double the existing line. A gentler gradient was used and this passes through the hill at the lower level, its exit being behind and below the Permanent Way hut visible in the background (see plate 152). The gradient of the 'down' line can be seen on the post against the engine, 1 in 80 to Patchway up the hill and 1 in 90 down through the tunnel. It was on this latter stretch that on the opening day of the B & SWUR an inaugural 'up' train stalled in the tunnel, with something in the order of 1,500 people crammed into 21 broad gauge coaches!

160. With Ashley Hill station in the background, No. 4068 again eases down the hill towards Narroways Junction. This is recorded as a 'down' north to west train and if so it has been enlarged with extra coaches from that shown in the Working Timetable. No. 4068 *Llanthony Abbey*, one of the 'Stars' built after the Great War, was to be withdrawn within a couple of years, to reappear as a member of the 'Castle' class and renumbered No. 5088. These 1920s-built engines were always a little different from their predecessors, probably due to Collett's influence, the last of them appeared not long before *Caerphilly Castle*. Certainly these later 'Stars' had none of the elegance of the earlier engines and when coupled to the large tender and with altered detail as here, looked more akin to the 'Castles'. This engine had the Collett 4,000 gallon tender attached during October 1935. The two leading coaches are brake composites on a Birkenhead – Plymouth working. The first is one of the 1934 vehicles which were a compromise between old and new styles. Early designs had a door to each compartment even on the corridor side whilst later on these were altered to end doors only. The E148s bridged the difference with a door per compartment on that side but on the corridor side every other door was omitted, both sides of these vehicles can be seen in plate 59 in Volume 1. The next vehicle is a Toplight. On the 'up' main line is a long sand drag with, adjacent to the sixth coach, a catch point. In the event of a vehicle becoming detached and rolling back down the 1 in 75 bank towards the junction, it would run through the catch point and into the two sand-filled channels, so slowing it down and bringing it to a stand. One wonders why the 'up' relief was not similarly protected, only a catch point immediately before the junction being provided.

161. The 5.15 p.m. Bristol – Paddington (4.35 p.m. from Weston-Super-Mare) ascends the hill away from Ashley Hill station on its journey out of Bristol. This section was the original single line opened in 1863 by the erstwhile Bristol and South Wales Union Railway. It was converted to standard gauge ten years later and doubled in 1886 with the opening of the Severn Tunnel, forming the main South Wales to London line. The opening of the South Wales and Bristol direct (or Badminton route), in 1903, reduced the South Wales traffic to either cross-country or local trains but the amount of traffic was still sufficient for the line to be quadrupled in 1933. This train is running on the new section. No. 4042 *Prince Albert* (named after the future King George VI) has a mixed rake of coaches. The first three are standard Collett designs of the 1920s, the next vehicle is one of the 70′ Dreadnought diners, this of diagram H11, followed by a Toplight and another Collett. The last three are also 70′ coaches but of the 'Concertina' type, the first being a composite, with most interestingly two slip coaches of diagram F13 attached to the rear. These are on slip coach working No 7 and No 18. The last vehicle (No 18) slips at Swindon and the next (No 7) at Reading.

162. A delightful photograph of a mixed train of GW and Southern Railway carriages in use on this Cardiff – Brighton express. It is passing the quarry at Foxes Wood just south-east of Bristol, on the Bath line. The train is, as one might expect for this secondary route, composed of various types of coaches of equally varying vintage. The Southern Railway stock are former LSWR 'Ironclad's' with their curiously distinctive 'Dreadnought' bogies. Some more of these vehicles were built after 1923 but had a different form of bogie fitted. The engine is one of the legendary 'Saints'. The first of this class was, if one discounts the prototype No. 100 (later 2900 *William Dean*), the remarkable No. 98 and could be described as Britain's first modern locomotive. All of Churchward's genius and design skills went into these locomotives which were to be the forerunners of many later classes, indeed the 'Hall' class began with an altered 'Saint'. This example is No. 2913 *Saint Andrew* from Bristol's Bath Road shed. Built in 1907 it was among the first to be superheated. Like the 'Stars' these engines were down graded with the introduction of newer and bigger 4-cylinder locomotives during the latter half of the 1920s and early 1930s, moving away from sheds like Old Oak Common and in turn displacing other still older engines on trains such as we see here. The leading coach, a steel panelled toplight third is just passing over the beginning of the troughs on the 'up' line. It is quite probable that *Saint Andrew* will replenish its tender tank here as these trains ran via Stapleton Road and Somerset Junction, avoiding Temple Meads Station at Bristol and a lengthy stop. This same stock can be seen in plate No. 32 in Volume 1.

163. An 'up' express, the 11.45 a.m. Bristol–Paddington, climbs the 1 in 75 gradient out of Bristol, passing Ashley Hill station and crossing Muller Road. Beneath the engine is the long sand drag put in as a protection against breakaways. No. 4028 *Roumanian Monarch* was built in 1909 as *King John* but with the advent of the 'King' class, it, along with several others, was renamed, this as *The Roumanian Monarch* in July 1927, the 'The' being removed in October. During World War II Roumania fought on the side of the Axis, so the name was removed, the engine did not have it replaced and so ran nameless until withdrawal. The train is a mix of Collett and Churchward designs, the most prominent being the articulated dining set in the middle of the train. High on the hill, partly hidden, is the Muller Orphanage, now the College of Technology.

164. 'Star' class 4-6-0 No. 4055 *Princess Sophia* pulls a freight train through Ashley Hill station and over Muller Road. The 'Star' class engines were used frequently on freight trains at this period and one can almost hear *Princess Sophia*, of Bath Road Shed, lift this early morning train up towards Filton Junction. Apart from the smoke drifting from the houses below Mullers Orphanage on the hill, No. 4055 appears to be the only moving thing. Notice the variety and periods of the wagons and vans in the train which is over 50 wagons long, including some SR round-ended types.

165. When we first saw this photograph we thought that the train had stalled, however, it may be that it is waiting for a banker. We have been told that it was common for the train, instead of picking up the banker at Stapleton Road (in the background), for it to pull up the hill and wait. There is a wisp of smoke at the rear of the train and the fireman is on the tender top looking back. Mr. Soole's records show this to be a west to north express, probably the 8.45 a.m. from Plymouth, the first coach a through working from Plymouth to Glasgow. Taken at 12.32 p.m. on August 12th, 1933, he also records the banker as a 'new 0-6-0'. The train is made up of some 14 coaches, mostly of LMS origin. Unfortunately the formation cannot be identified although a number of them are former LNWR vehicles. Certainly, at this moment in time, No. 5934 *Kneller Hall* was virtually new, only being a couple of months old having been completed in June 1933. The scene is Narroways Junction with the main lines on the left and the tracks to Avonmouth to the right.

166. A South Wales-bound freight threads the pointwork as it crosses from the main to the slow line on the climb away from Stapleton Road station, passing Narroways Junction. The tracks to the right go down to Avonmouth over the LMS-GWR line through Clifton and the Avon Gorge. Taken on July 20th 1933 at 2.35 p.m., the train is only travelling at about 15 mph at this point. A freight of this magnitude would normally be banked to Filton, however, with the train being composed of mostly empty wagons it appears that the '28XX' will be able to manage on its own. It is possible that this train is an empty Salisbury – South Wales working which has joined the main line at Dr. Day's Bridge Junction, the reason for it crossing to the slow line. No. 2869, built in November 1918, was allocated to Severn Tunnel Junction at this time, so is working home with the 'H' class goods. The new (1933) quad-rupled section can be seen to the left, although the section from the junction through to Dr. Day's Bridge Junction, was completed in 1891.

167. We see Stapleton Road station with 'Castle' class 4-6-0 No. 5030 *Shireburn Castle* pulling away with a 'B' set on a running-in turn, an evening Swindon – Bristol local. No. 5030 was normally based at Cardiff Canton shed and would return there after these trials and any subsequent adjustments. The train is on the 'down' relief and is crossing the bridge over St. Marks Road. The long wooden platform extensions were built in 1917.

168. One of the mighty 'King' class engines, No. 6009 *King Charles II*, stands in Stapleton Road station with a 'down' local. This is an ex-works running-in turn from Swindon often used by the Works to prove their efforts before returning the locomotive to its home shed. When satisfied, No. 6009 will be returned to Old Oak Common, the only shed it was ever allocated to. The step on the smokebox door was a new feature introduced in the early 1930s, probably added to assist the fireman when fitting the lamp when it was on top of the smokebox. However, they then moved the lampbracket to the door as seen. Behind the locomotive is a 'B' set, comprising two close-coupled brake composites, these of diagram E140 and a van. Stapleton Road was an important station in the area as a number of trains stopped here as they passed through Bristol eastwards and not calling at Temple Meads. When the Severn Tunnel was opened and before the direct route via Badminton was built, this was the main station for trains calling at Bristol on their way to and from South Wales.

171. The frontage and forecourt of Bristol Temple Meads taken during 1937. This is one of a series of photographs which show inside, out and the approaches to this lovely station. This is the entrance of the 1878 building designed by Sir Matthew Digby Wyatt, who had worked with Brunel on the construction of Paddington station. Temple Meads was a joint station, the partners being the Bristol & Exeter Railway, the Great Western and the Midland Railway. The GW was the principle partner and had taken over the B & ER in 1876 whilst the station was under construction. The three companies each had a seperate entrance and booking hall, the Midland to the left, Bristol & Exeter in the centre and the Great Western on the right. Two schemes were drawn for the 100 foot central tower, one with and the other without the spire. When the station was bombed in January 1941, the entrance was hit by an incendiary which gutted the booking area, the spire being burnt down and not subseqently replaced. The stone facade survived and the tower, minus spire, still stands today. The canopies around the front have been accredited to Francis Fox of the B & ER, who assisted Digby Wyatt in the design. To the left can be seen the extension to Brunel's original terminus, while to the right is the curved roof of the 1878 station. The motor cars and taxis are worth the photograph in themselves. There are Austins, Morris's, Humbers, Rovers, a Buick and an Armstrong Siddeley, today as evocative to the motoring enthusiast as the steam engines are to railwaymen. Most of these names have disappeared, along with their railway counterpart. Notice the boards advertising 'Puritan Soap' and the workman on his trestle repairing the canopy.

Opposite page top:
169. An evening train from Keysham of some ten coaches leaves Stapleton Road and begins the ascent to Narroways Junction where it will take the route via Clifton and the tunnel under the downs to Avonmouth. The tracks on which Mr. Soole is standing are level so it is possible to appreciate the inclination of 1 in 75 at this point, beginning from under the fourth coach. The little engine certainly looks as if it is working hard which it will need to for this short climb. No. 5506 was built in 1927 but had a relatively short life of just over 30 years, diesels making many of these fine little locomotives redundant. The tall signal with the small calling-on arm is for the 'down' relief, set over from its normal position for clearance purposes.

Opposite page bottom:
170. One of Churchwards lovely small Prairie tank engines, No. 5540, pulls away from Stapleton Road with an 'up' local, probably to Avonmouth. It is running on the 'up' relief as an express crosses the 1891 girder bridges in the background on the 'up' main line. This engine was resident at Bath Road for a number of years, working local trains in the district. Built in 1928 No. 5540 eventually succumbed to dieselisation in 1960. The original design of these engines appeared in 1906 but construction continued up until 1929 when the final batch of one hundred, enlarged versions of which No. 5540 was one, was completed. They were very useful little engines found all over the system but remembered better for their monopoly of many branch lines than for the work being done here. The train is composed of a 'B' set, i.e. two brake composites close-coupled in the middle. These are of diagram E145 and are numbered 6193 and 6199 which was formed as Bristol Division Train No. 27 in July 1936. The trackwork in the foreground, which includes a double compound, is part of Stapleton's Goods Yard.

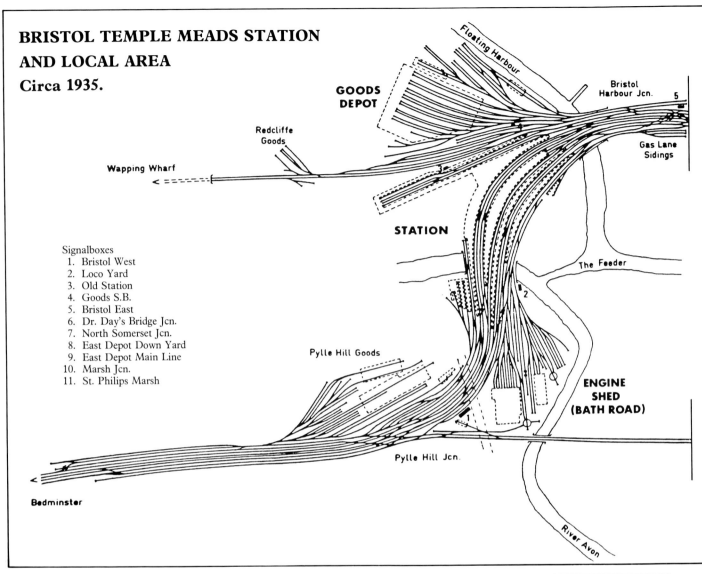

BRISTOL TEMPLE MEADS STATION
AND LOCAL AREA
Circa 1935.

Signalboxes
1. Bristol West
2. Loco Yard
3. Old Station
4. Goods S.B.
5. Bristol East
6. Dr. Day's Bridge Jcn.
7. North Somerset Jcn.
8. East Depot Down Yard
9. East Depot Main Line
10. Marsh Jcn.
11. St. Philips Marsh

GOODS DEPOT

Floating Harbour

Bristol Harbour Jcn.

Gas Lane Sidings

Redcliffe Goods

Wapping Wharf

STATION

The Feeder

Pylle Hill Goods

ENGINE SHED (BATH ROAD)

Pylle Hill Jcn.

Bedminster

River Avon

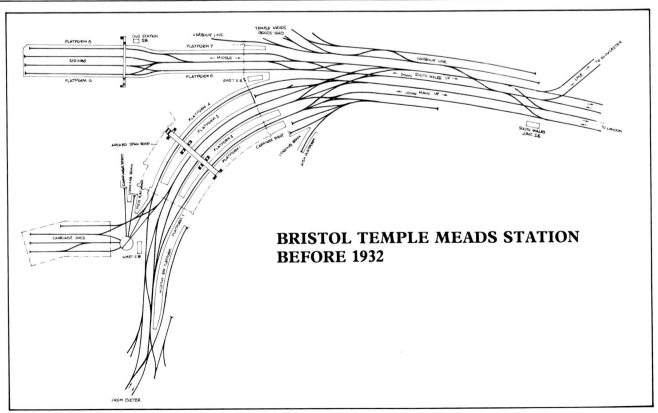

BRISTOL TEMPLE MEADS STATION
BEFORE 1932

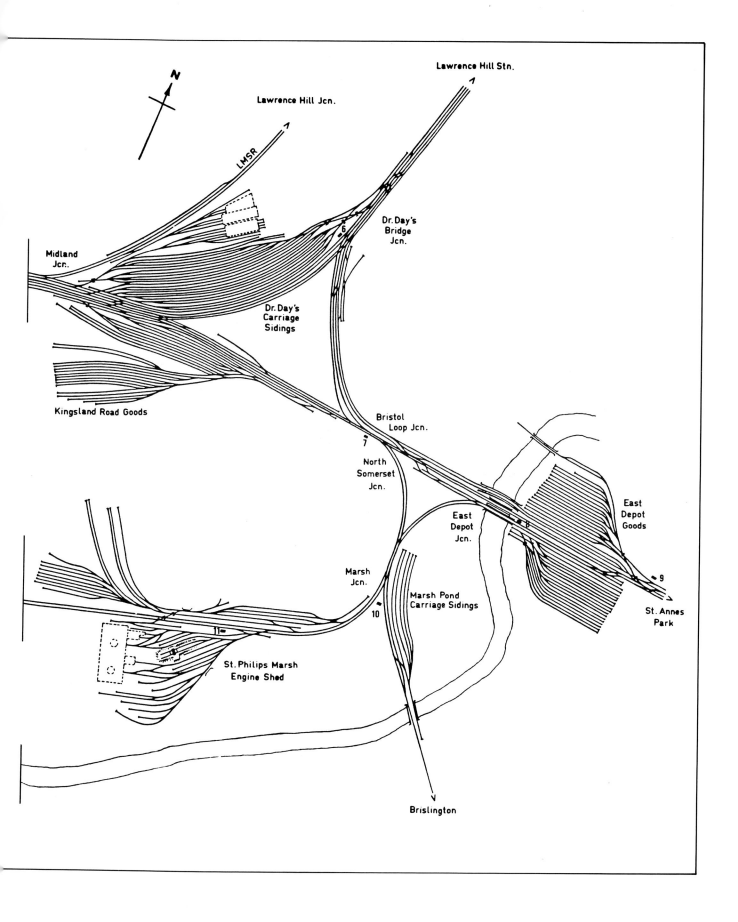

172. This is a view of Temple Meads taken from Platform 9 in a southerly direction. The 125 ft. span of Digby Wyatts overall train shed, which was completed in 1878 when the modern Temple Meads was built, is clearly seen. During the 1930s the interior was altered entirely, while outside, the station was considerably enlarged with new platforms being added. The original internal layout of the 1870s was altered slightly after the abandonment of the Broad Gauge in 1892 to that of two single through roads with platforms either side and a double track running between them. Although there were only four platforms, there were actually six platform faces. It was considered inadequate even when first laid down, but it was to be a bottleneck for nearly sixty years until work commenced in 1930 to ease what was becoming a severe handicap to train working in the area. Beyond the end of the older building, with its soot-stained screen, can be seen the canopies of the new platforms (a local train stands at Platform 10).

173. In a view from across the River Avon looking into the south end of Temple Meads station, it is possible to see many of the rebuilt areas. The new bridge in the foreground was put up during 1933 when a large new section of bridging was put across the river to enable the whole of the station throat, new platform, through lines and new engine shed roads to be laid in. The original width was for three tracks and one platform, with the new one having three platforms and fourteen tracks with elbow-room. The long platform at which the 'Castle'-hauled express stands is No. 5 and 4. Behind this is the 1934-built repair shop and coal stage and to its right, the locomotive sheds built at the same time on the site of the old Bristol and Exeter Railway Works. In the foreground are the loading banks with that on the left having a LNER 5 plank, a GW horse-box, two LMS vans and a GW Siphon at the far end. The other dock has two siphons standing in it, the nearer a Siphon G and beyond it the taller Siphon H.

174. Here we see the northern end of Temple Meads Station and its immediate approaches, viewed from the roof of East signalbox. In the station a train awaits departure, its engine an LMS 'Jubilee' class. The tracks from left to right are Gas Lane Siding, 'down' relief, 'down' main, 'up' main, 'up' relief and 'up' and 'down' relief, those on the extreme right running behind the building are head shunts. The pointwork from the 'up' and 'down' relief cross to the right to Bristol Harbour Junction, which leads to the harbour, Redcliffe goods yard and Temple Meads Goods Depot which is the large shed complex in the distance. The large black shed to the right on the lower level is the former Midland Railway barge/railway transhipment shed on Avonside Wharf. The stretch of water which runs beneath the bridge section is the floating harbour, the non-tidal harbour of Bristol controlled by lock-gates. The two passenger brake vans in the Gas Lane Siding are a GWR K22 van in brown livery and a former LNWR Diagram 375 vehicle. Two spires dominate the scene, that on the right belonging to the familiar St. Mary Redcliffe, that on the left above the station roof, is the clock tower over the main booking hall.

175. An 'up' express departs from Temple Meads station, hauled by Exeter's No. 5026 *Cricceith Castle*. This 'Castle' was among those which were revitalised in the twilight of their lives when equipped with double chimneys and new super-heaters, eventually being transferred and ending their day under the LMR. On the right can be seen the end of a brown painted passenger brake van with a roof headboard, the last word of which is Cardiff, coupled to the brake end of a coach. This is one of a pair, comprising a 'B' Set, branded Bristol Division No. 7 and made up of diagram E116 brake composites 7625 and 7626.

176. An interesting photograph, one of a number taken at the same time showing the streamlined 'Castle' No. 5005 *Manorbier Castle* starting away from No. 9 platform of Temple Meads, Bristol with an 'up' express. As the locomotive has all its fairings in place, the picture can be dated as having been taken between March and September 1935, when the tender cowl and the front end streamlining around the footplate and cylinders was removed. Mr. Collett's concept of removing the areas of resistance can be clearly seen here, even if most people feel it did nothing for the classic lines of the 'Castle'. The leading coach in the train is a rebuilt ex-World War I ambulance train vehicle, which had started life as a wooden panelled Toplight brake third. When refurbished the vehicle was steel panelled without toplights, and became diagram D88.

177. Emerging into the sunlight, an Old Oak Common-based 'Castle' No. 4037 departs from under the roof of Bristol Temple Meads station on a London bound train. On the platform, work has still not been completed after the removal of the old East signalbox, and the erection of the new platform canopies. However, gone are the semaphore signals and the colour light signals are now operational as work nears completion after five years or so to totally re-model and enlarge this famous station. Beyond, in Wyatts extension of Brunels original terminus, a local train awaits departure. This view was taken some two years after that above, making an interesting comparison. This famous engine was built in 1910 as a member of the 'Star' class and named *Queen Philippa*. In 1926 it was withdrawn and rebuilt into a member of the 'Castle' class, retaining its old identity. However, early in 1937 it was renamed *The South Wales Borderers* and fitted with the regimental plaque seen here on the splasher. It was eventually withdrawn in 1962 after a gallant 52 years of main line service during which it attained the highest mileage of any Great Western engine, over 2,400,000 miles.

178. Taken on the 28th April 1937 a special excursion waits to leave Platform 6 at Temple Meads. Beautifully clean, No. 4081 *Warwick Castle* waits to leave with a special to Slough then to Pinewood Studios the capital of the British movie industry. These trains were supposedly very popular with the ordinary public, giving them a glimpse into a world, far removed from the everyday existence of the masses, trying to break out of the grips of the depression. It is probable that *Warwick Castle* has just been through the works at Swindon. It is known that up until the end of 1936 this engine had the upper lampbracket on top of the smokebox – the last of the 'Castles' with this feature. It has also been fitted with a speedometer. The leading coach is one of those specially designed for through working over other companies routes such as Cardiff – York and Bristol – Aberdeen for which they were equipped with Westinghouse brake pipes. Built in 1896 to diagram E48 eight were constructed but one was destroyed at Llanelly in 1904. Later some of their diagrams changed as alterations affected the remaining seven, the one seen here is classified as E105.

179. This photograph shows '5800' class No. 5800 shunting at the west end of Bristols Temple Meads and was taken prior to the rebuilding of the early 1930s, in fact, at 3.25 p.m. on June 21st 1933. At the right above the train is Bristol West signalbox which was removed in April 1934 to make way for the alterations. The wooden platform was added in 1892 to allow longer trains on the 'down' main line. The locomotive and train is standing on the 'up' main line where it passes over the River Avon on a bridge which had been a bottle-neck until its rebuilding. No. 5800 is quite new here, having only been completed in the January of 1933. It was the first engine of the non-auto fitted class of 0-4-2Ts, which were derived from the '4800' (later '1400') class. Above the engine is the roof of the original Bristol & Exeter Railway building. In front of this is the newly erected GPO building, built on the site of the B & E's carriage sheds.

180. An 'up' express slows as it approaches Bristol West and the curve into Temple Meads. The train is running on the relief line, and is headed by No. 5019 *Treago Castle*. The coaches are mostly of GW origin with a number of LMS vehicles. This is the 8.45 a.m. Plymouth to Crewe which continued on from Bristol at 12.23 p.m. The leading coach is a brake composite running from Plymouth to Birkenhead. Next is a dining car attached at Weston-Super-Mare for Shrewsbury, this then worked empty to Wolverhampton returning to Weston the following day on the 7.05 a.m. Wolverhampton to Bristol and forward from there. The next coach is a GW brake composite working from Plymouth to Glasgow. Following are three LMS coaches which alternated daily with three GWR vehicles running between Plymouth and Liverpool. The next five GW coaches are attached at Newton Abbot from Paignton, the first two going to Manchester and the last three to Bradford. Behind the engine is a GW 'TOAD' brakevan, an LNER van No. 51910 and, with the end only visible, GW 'OPEN C' No. 25025 built to diagram O8. In the background is the area known as Bedminster, the station is just along to the left, towards the WD and HO Wills factory. This area received a lot of bomb damage in World War II.

181. Waiting rather impatiently for his turn for platform space the driver of No. 5011 *Tintagel Castle* watches the signals intently. This engine spent most of its GW career in the Newton Abbot division going there new in 1927 and was still there in 1947, alternating between Newton Abbot and Laira sheds. This was the penultimate 'Castle' fitted with the old inside cylinder casing. It has a speedometer and the upper lampbracket moved, these being about the only modifications ever made to these engines (although it came out with a small tender). No. 5011 lasted until 1962 running nearly 1¼ million miles. Behind the tender is a horsebox of diagram N13, presumably occupied as the grooms droplight is open. In the background, in front of the Pyle Hill Goods Depot, is a Clerestory corridor third which has had rather a lot of patching on the body sides.

182. No. 2933 *Bibury Court*, a member of the splendid 'Saint' class, stands opposite Bristol West signalbox with its train. The engine carries a 'B' headcode, used to denote an ordinary passenger train but this might well be an empty stock train coming in from Malago Vale carriage sidings as there are no passengers in sight. If this is correct, the locomotive has the wrong headcode – a seemingly not infrequent occurrence! Most of the carriages are very modern and the third coach is a non-corridor type of note. Built to diagram D117 in 1934, these were the first vehicles to be designed with the double doors to the van section fitted with only one window, that in the left-hand door. Previous to this, both doors had windows – with droplights fitted. *Bibury Court* (pronounced Bi-burry) was named after part of the estate belonging to Lord Shelbourne. The village of Bibury, which was described as 'the most beautiful village in England' by William Morris, the 19th century artist and poet, is in the Cotswolds near Cirencester. As far as we have been able to establish, Lord Shelbourne had no connections with the GWR.

183. Looking like the ramparts of a medieval castle, the houses of Richmond Street dominate the view south west of Temple Meads station. An unidentified 'Hall' (the sun is reflecting on name and numberplates) stands waiting to enter the station, the fireman resting, watching Mr. Soole at work. This represents what might be called the classic train of the Collett era. The Siphon G has roof label brackets and is gas lit while the rest of the stock, unusually, is from one period. Designed by Collett and built some 10 years before, these vehicles were allocated to 6-coach sets, but they were soon dispersed. However, apart from being one third class coach short, this is what was envisaged.

184. No. 5013 *Abergavenny Castle*, is seen at the head of the midday Penzance to Crewe train as it enters Bristol past Pyle Hill Goods Depot in the early evening. This was the first of the 'Castle' class built with the modified cover over the inside cylinders and with a redesigned firebox. Behind the tender is a GW Travelling Post Office van of diagram L22 No. 799, which was allocated for this working. This van was detached at Bristol along with the first coach. Next follows a pair of LMS vehicles, both brake composites but of totally different styles. The first of these is an LMS-built coach of Diagram 1720 whilst the other is an unidentified vehicle. The rest, commencing with the inside framed Siphon G, are all GW coaches, going to either Liverpool or Manchester with a single coach for Glasgow. On the right is a pannier tank engine, working in the goods yard. A line of wagons can also be seen.

185. Three trains pass near Pyle Hill Goods Depot, the goods train on the right is taking the avoiding lines which lead through to Dr. Day's Junction via St. Philips Marsh. On the left the rear of an 'up' passenger train can be seen heading into Bristol Temple Meads on the relief lines. In the centre a resplendant No. 6003 *King George IV* from Old Oak Common heads a 'down' express to the West, her driver checking his train. Most of the coaches are 70′ vehicles including the first, a Toplight brake third of diagram D51. This is a left-hand van (viewed from the corridor-side) and has the short-lived multi-bar system of underframing. The third coach in the 'down' express is the unique 'Dreadnought' dining car of diagram H11. This is in fact the best photograph of this vehicle in the series. Compare the bogie wheelbase on this vehicle with the coaches on either side which have 7′ and 9′ bogies. These experimental bogies were removed from No. 9505 in August 1939, when the original type of 6-wheel bogies were restored.

186. Mr. Soole records this as the 11.15 a.m. Paddington – Weston-Super-Mare, hauled by No. 4084 *Aberystwyth Castle* from Old Oak Common shed which, by this late 1937 period, still retains the earlier tender crest and insignia, superseded in 1934 by the circular logo. This was the first 'Castle' fitted with the Automatic Train Control from new. It was to feature among the earlier withdrawals and had the lowest mileage from among the first batches. The leading coach is a 1937-built kitchen car of which there were six, numbered 9663-68 to diagram H54. Through the bridge, erected in 1933 when the station approaches were enlarged, can be seen a '55XX' attached to the Bristol Mess and Tool riding vans, Nos. 90 and 91.

187. Two trains pass in the cutting at Long Ashton on April 6th 1933, at 1.30 p.m. The 'up' train is pulled by No. 6015 *King Richard III* and is composed of a mixture of 57' and 70' stock. The first, fresh from a recent overhaul, is a slip coach to diagram F20 on working No. 16, which returns it to Paddington ready for the following day. The train is the 9.50 a.m. Ilfracombe – Bristol picking up coaches at Barnstaple Junction and Taunton, including the dining car. From Bristol, which it leaves at 1.45 p.m., the train runs via Bath, where further coaches were added before continuing to London. The next morning the slip returns to Ilfracombe but via the Berks & Hants line, being slipped in company with a brake composite from the 'down' Cornish Riviera Express at Taunton on slip working No. 15. Three vehicles were allocated for this slip working during this period, two being in use daily out and back. These were Nos. 6962, 6963 and 6964, all single ended coaches with a gangway at the other end. The 'down' train, the 11.15 a.m. from Paddington to Weston-Super-Mare, has a more uniform rake of carriages most of which are 1929 'Riviera' vehicles with the exception of the third from rear, which is a 70' Dreadnought diner. All of these are of the wide bodied style, 9'7" across the waist, of limited route availability which could usually only be used on former broad gauge routes.

190. A lovely wintery scene showing a 'down' local train as it emerges from the cutting at Long Ashton. The shadows cast by the trees and smoke, aided by the skeletal form of the leafless trees and overhead telegraph wires, combine to frame the scene. One of Churchward's original '43XX' class, No. 4365, of the fifth batch completed in July 1915, is in sparkling condition and obviously has recently been into the workshops. During the mid-thirties this engine was at Weymouth, Westbury and Swindon sheds. From what may be discerned of the train itself, through the drifting smoke, it comprises a 'B' set, of diagram E140 and two third class coaches. A lovely photograph.

Opposite page top:
188. An 'up' express runs between Flax Bourton and Long Ashton on a rather misty day. At its head is No. 4022 *Belgian Monarch* from Bristol Bath Road Shed. Originally built in 1909 it was named *King William* until June 1927 when, with the advent of the 'King' class, its name was removed and *The Belgian Monarch* fitted. After a few months the 'The' was removed. Eventually, during May 1940, it lost this name altogether and thereafter ran nameless until withdrawal in 1952. The tender, of Churchward design and 3,500 gallon capacity, ran with No. 4022 from August 1935 until July 1939. The train is comprised of 14 vehicles, all very different from each other. The front coach is one of the small saloons introduced for private hire by families. Most railways had many types of similar vehicles, including the Great Western, but following the recession and then the depression after the Great War, this traffic fell away and of the forty of these saloons built during the 1890s, to diagram G20, only a dozen or so remained by 1937. Next to this, in contrast, is a very modern third class coach from the excursion sets introduced only in this year. Gone are compartments and corridors and many outer doors and instead we see a coach which would not be out of place today. Two clerestories follow, one a GW vehicle, diagram C17, with an ex-Midland Railway composite of Bain design next to it. Note the difference in roof heights.

Opposite page bottom:
189. An 'up' express sweeps under the Ashton Brook aqueduct at Long Ashton. This is recorded as a west to north train and if so the first two coaches, both brake composites, will travel on from Crewe to other destinations. The locomotive is No. 2933 *Bibury Court* completed in 1911. During the early twenties it ran for a couple of years with the chimney moved forward (by about 12 inches) in one of a number of experiments being tried out on engines of both 'Saint' and 'Star' classes. A short safety valve cover has been fitted and the lamp bracket moved. As with the 'Star' class, these fine engines had been demoted to cross country services, having disappeared from the top-link duties and the sheds at Paddington and in the West Country. They themselves had displaced other engines such as the 'County' and outside-framed 4-4-0s which were withdrawn. They were always considered as fine locomotives and one of Churchward's outstanding designs, *Bibury Court* lasting for over forty years. Notice the distant signal with its sighting board against the aqueduct, the board having a dark background to show the yellow arm more clearly. The Courts of the 'Saint' class began the tradition which was to serve the GWR well in providing a virtual endless list of buildings to name their engines and classes after. The 'Abbeys' came next, followed by the 'Castles', 'Halls', 'Granges' and 'Manors'. It was said the next class was to have been the 'Cathedrals'.

191. No. 5008 *Raglan Castle* heads towards Bristol, passing Long Ashton with an 'up' express. It is the 1.30 p.m. Taunton – Paddington due in at 5.35 p.m. No. 5008 was allocated to Paddington for a number of years from the mid 1930s so it is working home with this train. When first completed in 1927 it was sent new to Laira. This engine was one of two 'Castles' equipped with experimental speedometers in 1933 but when seen here in 1937, it has received a standard BTH unit. Behind the tender is a passenger brake van, which should be No. 75 of diagram K40 which was branded for this train, working from Plymouth. This van returned direct to Plymouth on the 12.50 a.m. newspaper train to the West of England. The next pair were attached at Weston-Super-Mare and are a composite and refreshment car, in reality a 57′ dining car. The following seven coaches are all from Taunton though the last three, which includes a Siphon G (replacing a 70′ newspaper van) at the rear are detached at Swindon but were forwarded to Paddington on a later train.

192. We see here a magnificent picture of a GWR train in the late 1930s. The 9-coach train is in the beautiful countryside of Somerset and its cream and brown coaches (never did the Great Western refer to the colours as 'chocolate and cream') are offset by the engine's green and black, with copper and brasswork. Bristol-based 4-6-0 No. 5048 *Cranbrook Castle*, which is soon to be renamed *Earl of Devon*, in August 1937, is photographed with a 'down' express near Long Ashton. The station is visible through the bridge to the rear. The train is most likely the 11.15 a.m. Paddington – Weston-Super-Mare, at least for the leading six coaches. The three additions to the rear may be just extras attached at Bristol. This train ran with a slip portion at the rear to Didcot where the slip and two coaches were detached – part of slip coach working No. 13 – for Oxford.

193. An 'up' Weston-Super-Mare – Bristol stopping train but with an express headcode, leaves Flax Bourton station behind and approaches the short tunnel of the same name. Mr. Soole was standing on the footbridge, a relic from broad gauge days, to take this view, the train passing the site of the former broad gauge station. The culvert to the left is where the original 'down' platform building stood. The remains of the footpaths down to the platforms can be seen in the embankments on either side. On the right, in front of the engine, can be seen Mile Post 124, another item left from the broad gauge period. The train, hauled by a member of the 'Saint' class, No. 2955 *Tortworth Court*, is seen here on July 29th 1933 at 1.37 p.m. In January of the following year, the engine was fitted with outside steam pipes, when new cylinders were fitted. The leading van has had its projections (never did the GW call them duckets) removed, altering its diagram from K4 to K30. The vehicle has recently had a repaint, its roof still showing white. Tortworth Court was owned by the Earl of Ducie (this title one of those affixed to the 'Earl' class – which later were transferred to a batch of 'Castles'). It stands in Gloucestershire to the north of Bristol.

194. Collett 0-6-0 No. 2268 draws into Flax Bourton station with a very interesting Temple Meads – Weston local train. The stock behind the engine is not the type usually seen by 1933 on scheduled trains and is made up of what appears to be a close-coupled set of 8 or 9 vehicles. These rakes of coaches were originally used in the city areas as suburban commuter trains. By this time many had been split, the vehicles being used separately. The leading two vehicles are an outside-framed Siphon and a 4-wheeled coach of an earlier vintage than the set. Built in June 1930, No. 2268 was one of the earliest members of what was eventually to be the final design of 0-6-0 to be constructed in this country. The 0-6-0 had been the standard freight engine from the earliest days of railways in Britain. Collett designed these locomotives as replacements for the ageing Dean and Armstrong standard goods. Indeed they were only a modernised Dean with a modern coned boiler, giving them a higher tractive effort and a full cab. Even the tenders sometimes came from withdrawn engines. Note the litter, probably thrown from passing trains. Mr. Soole records the date as August 15th 1933 and notes the train is 17 minutes late, the time being 2.45 p.m.

195. Flax Bourton station is the setting as a 'down' express hurries through at about 50 mph in June 1933. This is a Birmingham to Plymouth train which left Bristol at 1.45 p.m. Although appearing deserted, the station is in a very clean and tidy condition, with all its fire buckets in place. Beyond this is the hill through which passes Flax Bourton Tunnel. The remains of a Roman settlement lay almost above the tunnel, perhaps this being the reason why the Bristol & Exeter Railway, who built the line, tunneled rather than opened it out into a cutting. The engine is 4-6-0 No. 5014 *Goodrich Castle* which is only about twelve months old. This was the second of the 'Castle' class to be fitted with a fire-iron tunnel from new, as well as the altered casing over the inside cylinders.

196. The 9.55 a.m. from Ilfracombe speeds into Flax Bourton station at 1.34 p.m. on June 21st 1933. It is hauled by No. 6018 *King Henry VI* from Newton Abbot shed and is travelling at about 60 mph. The ground and platforms are wet from a recent shower, this view being taken some 29 minutes before that above, Mr. Soole recorded. He also mentions that it was his birthday (he was 20 years old). The arrangement of the signalbox set back as it is, is unusual, the path to the station passing in front of it. The fact that the bend curves to the left for a long distance either side of the station must have given the signalmen a very poor view of approaching trains, particularly those from the north. The goods yard on the right is hidden by No. 6018's exhaust.

197. A member of the 'Saint' class slows as it approaches Uphill Junction where it will take the loop line into Weston-Super-Mare. This is a Taunton – Bristol train which on arrival will form the 3.15 p.m. Bristol – Paddington express. The time, Mr. Soole records, is 2.33 p.m. on August 4th 1933. Built in 1911, No. 2940 *Dorney Court* has not been altered a great deal apart from a short safety valve cover and the front top lamp bracket moved to the smokebox. The train, as far as can be discerned, is made up of Churchward's 70′ Toplight stock and a Concertina. The crew have seen Mr. Soole and have moved across to watch him and the signals for the junction ahead. Behind the train is a magnificent overbridge, the long arch being a feature of the bridges on this section of the line, as can be seen elsewhere in this book. This particular bridge is reputedly 75 feet above the track. This famous cutting slices through the western end of the Mendip Hills, near to the point where they jut out into the Bristol Channel. *Dorney Court* was named after the famous Manor house which has been in the ownership of the Palmer family for over 350 years. It is situated in Buckinghamshire, not far from Windsor.

198. Bristol Bath Road shed on a misty, dismal day with 'Star' class No. 4064 *Reading Abbey* standing just outside the doors. Beyond is the still new-looking coal stage, opened, with the rest of the buildings, in 1934. This replaced the old Bristol and Exeter works and sheds, demolished during 1933 to make way for the new Bath Road complex constructed as part of the Railway Development Scheme of 1929. No. 4064 was built at the end of 1922 and was withdrawn in February 1937. It re-emerged in the guise of a member of the 'Castle' class, renumbered to No. 5084 but retaining its name. How much of the original engine was re-used (certainly the frames) or scrapped is not clear, but the GW always looked upon this and the others similarly and treated them as new locomotives, not rebuilds.

199. One of Armstrong's little 0-4-2Ts of the '517' class stands on a shed road at St. Philips Marsh in 1936. Built in March of 1876, No. 1163 saw many changes throughout its existence before finally being withdrawn in May 1946, a career of over 70 years. Probably its use was rather limited around Bristol but it may be seen working in plate 71 in Volume 1. These engines were originally designed as saddle tanks in 1868 but by the time No. 1163 was built at Wolverhampton, they were appearing as side tanks. This engine had its wheelbase extended in August 1895 and was fitted with a Belpaire boiler in May 1913. The first cabs were fitted in the 1880s, Swindon completing the job under Churchward, although by no means were the whole class treated. New Collett style bunkers appeared in the 1920s. No. 1163 was among a batch fitted with larger 800 gallon tanks after 1925. During Churchward's time, it was auto-fitted and painted in the livery matching the auto-coaches it ran with. Between 1930 and 1931, it had an ATC shoe and apparatus fitted (seen under the bunker). No. 1163 was amongst the last of the class withdrawn, (from Weymouth), being transferred there shortly after this picture was taken in 1936. It attained a fantastic mileage for such a little engine, over 1,650,000 miles. Note the letters SPM, indicating its shed, stencilled on the lamp on the footplate and the larger diameter buffer heads added for auto work.

200. A scene inside Bristol's St. Philips Marsh engine shed as an ex-M&SWJ Rly 0-6-0 No. 24, now GWR No. 1008, receives attention from a fitter who is working on a wash-out plug. The Midland & South Western had ten of these engines built by Beyer Peacock. This locomotive was constructed in 1899, taken over by the GWR in 1923 and rebuilt with No. 10 boiler to diagram A24 in March 1927. No. 1008 was transferred to Bristol in 1936 with two sister engines, Nos. 1011 and 1013, but was withdrawn in December of that same year, the others following during the next few months. It would appear that the tender has no markings at all on its sides. This particular engine was known to have worked on the Cheddar line but what other work or why indeed they were transferred is unclear.

201. A 'down' Bristol local takes the line to Filton behind a beautifully clean member of the 'Saint' class. In the background is Stoke Gifford West Junction and signalbox with a bracket signal protecting the pointwork of the junction and showing three equal home arms, one for each of the three routes. This train would have been signalled to proceed by the right-hand arm (as we look at it). The centre one is for the Avonmouth line and that on the left for the South Wales route. The locomotive is on a running-in turn from Swindon Works, loaned to the running department to enable the engine to be tested with local trips such as this. Obviously three coaches will not provide much of a test for No. 2928 *Saint Sebastian*, however, any faults should come to light. During its 41-year existence *Saint Sebastian* was usually found at one of the northern sheds, either Shrewsbury or Stafford Road. It was eventually withdrawn from Westbury shed in 1948. Behind the engine, the coaches are a Dean clerestory third, this one of over 200 similar vehicles, one of the largest single design of coach built by the Great Western, to diagram C10. The other two vehicles are a 'B' set. Note the demounted gangers trolley to the right, its wheels standing in front. The wooden hut is a temporary affair, not seen in other views of this location.

202. This photograph was taken sometime early in 1937 and shows a nearly new member of the '5101' class, No. 4119. This engine was completed in November 1936 and sent to Severn Tunnel Junction shed. It looks as though it is being used for banking duties and has perhaps been called upon to fill-in on this train. This was one of the standard tanks, all stemming from Churchward's No. 99 of 1903, which continued to be built until 1949 being useful engines for any sort of short distance work. The express is probably a Bristol – Cardiff train and has a mixture of coaches. The first pair are modern third class vehicles, the first being one of those 'between style' coaches with less doors on the corridor side, before the change to end doors only. The next coach of a slightly earlier and more conventional design has a pronounced lean to the compartment side (perhaps it's full!). The following coaches, all clerestories, appear to be a set of some kind and they have a 'Low Siphon' attached to the rear.

203. An unidentified member of the 'Castle' class from the 'Earl' series begins the climb out of Bristol of some three miles – two of which are at 1 in 75 – to Filton Junction in the summer of 1937. The train is the 'up' Bristolian which departs at 4.30 p.m., reaching Paddington at 6.15 p.m. The train was the 10.00 a.m. 'down' from London, which is sent to Malago Vale carriage sidings for cleaning and storing until 4.10 p.m. when it is worked back to Temple Meads for the return journey. The stock is, as one expects, a uniform set of modern coaches, the oldest of which is the buffet car built in 1934.

204. A superb action photograph of 'Star' class No. 4033 *Queen Victoria* at the head of a train storming over the summit of Filton incline. The train is the 11.45 a.m. Bristol – Paddington and includes an articulated dining car set. The engine is still in something like original condition, although the patches on the smokebox side indicate that the boiler has been fitted to an engine equipped with outside steam pipes. Allocated to Bristol, the engine will probably return with the 6.30 p.m. from London. The tender, of the 3,500 gallon Churchward type, was attached to No. 4033 from February 1936 until January 1937. The board on the right is to inform drivers of the requirement to stop down goods and mineral trains to allow the guard to pin down the brakes before descending the incline. These would remain pinned until Stapleton Road was reached.

205. 'Castle' class 4-6-0 No. 5012 *Berry Pomeroy Castle*, from Cardiff, hauls an 'up' express through Stoke Gifford yard in the summer of 1933. We can see in the sidings, from left to right, a number of vans and tank wagons with alongside of them a rake of engineering P diagram open wagons. Next is a line of open, general merchandise wagons loaded with what looks like sand, the first, GW No. 108105 is to diagram O22. Further along this same track are some loaded coal wagons. On the next-but-one is an interesting group of non-passenger coaching stock and horseboxes. The nearest vehicle is a former LSW brake van No. 86, built in 1896. This was later converted to departmental use, numbered 1345s, during 1938.

206. The fireman looks out as his engine prepares to set off out of the east end of the yard at Stoke Gifford. Built in 1929, No. 4941 *Llangedwyn Hall* was fitted with a mechanical lubricator in the early 'thirties and was shedded at Swindon. Its cylinders have the snifting valves set into the side, rather than the more usual position on the runningplate. Equipped with a Churchward 3,500 gallon tender at this time, it was one of the last to receive them when new, later engines receiving Collett types. The first van is an LNER vehicle with various brandings including Southampton and Sea Mills. Obviously, it is travelling from this latter destination, probably to wherever the ticket says.

207. A new 'Hall' class on its running-in turn from Swindon Works passes through the east end of the yard at Stoke Gifford. The train, an 'up' local from Bristol Temple Meads – Swindon, via Badminton, is seen here at 11.35 a.m. on August 14th 1933. No. 5940 *Whitbourne Hall* is in sparkling condition, as might be expected for a new engine, and has an easy task with a lightweight train. The engine was allocated to Stafford Road upon release from the Works. During 1934 it spent two months at Tyseley before moving to Oxley shed in the August. Behind the 4,000 gallon tender are two LNER perishable vans, a C10 clerestory third and a Toplight E82 brake composite. There are many items of note in the yard, particularly the large number of men above the last coach, either a track gang or the scene of a derailment?

208. At the junction of three different routes at the western end of Stoke Gifford Yard is a class 'H' freight from South Wales. The line on which it is running is the 'up' main curving round from Patchway, with the tracks down to Avonmouth passing between the telegraph pole and the centre tall home signal. To the left are the tracks running round to Filton and Bristol. Those three tall signals all protect their 'up' lines into the junction. The engine is one of the rebuilt 2-8-0T tank engines, this one, No. 7207, was formerly numbered 5282 and converted in October 1934.

209. A super photograph of the 11.45 p.m. Bristol – Paddington rounding the curve between Filton Junction and Stoke Gifford, early in 1936. The weak wintry sun lights up the subject showing the various types of carriages and the engine to advantage. This train reached Paddington at 1.45 p.m. and returned on the 6.30 p.m. London – Plymouth, attached to the rear. This started as an 11-coach train but the eight for Bristol were detached on arrival and seven added in their place. These latter included LMS coaches as well as GW vehicles, used for through workings from Birkenhead, Glasgow and Manchester to the West Country. The leading van third is one of the wider 1929 Riviera stock, this of the camera-shy design D108. The centre three are members of the 1925 articulated diner sets, soon to be altered. In charge is No. 4015 *Knight of St. John* built in early 1908 and one of the last of the 'Star' class to leave Old Oak Common.

210. Another rather confusing photograph which is claimed to show a north to west express. When the GWR introduced the original series of train identification numbers in July 1934 it allotted a batch for use at a station or district on trains starting there. The series commenced at 100, for trains ex-Paddington and ended at 799 for trains ex-South Wales. Specials or Boat Trains used an OXX number irrespective of origin. What 836 was allotted to is not known, but by this time, 1937, some changes to the original had taken place. What can be said is that the train is heading east near Stoke Gifford and has just passed through the Severn Tunnel. Pulling the train is one of the Great Western's best loved locomotives No. 4079 *Pendennis Castle*, built in 1924, the seventh of the class. It was this engine which, in 1925, was sent to the LNER, running with such stunning effect it totally outclassed their engines on their home territory. This influenced not only future LNER engines, but also those of the LMS. It is a great pity to record that although still extant, this engine now resides in Australia. At the time of this photograph No. 4079 was allocated to either Cardiff or Ebbw Junction (Newport), ending 1937 in its birthplace of Swindon. The leading vehicle is of interest. In the transition from Churchward Toplight to the Collett steel bodied standard stock with bow ends, some interim vehicles were built with flat ends and bogies/underframes similar to the last Toplights. In fact when originally painted they were given mock painted panelling to match the wooden bodied Toplights.

213. The 11.55 a.m. Paddington – Milford Haven express rounds the curve from Stoke Gifford to Patchway. The engine is No. 5039 *Rhuddlan Castle* built in June 1935 and is in fact older than the first three coaches. Of special note is the 'Dreadnought' diner which follows these three vehicles, it is No. 9505 of diagram H11. This coach was fitted with 11′6″ wheelbase, 4-wheeled 'American' bogies in place of its original 6-wheeled type. The equalising beam between the wheels was very deep and can be clearly seen here. These were experimental bogies fitted in January 1910 and removed, to be replaced by standard 12′6″ 6-wheel bogies, in August 1939. While lasting for so long, they can not have been considered any better than the original bogies since no further examples were constructed.

Opposite page top:
211. Heading homeward with a 'down' express, No. 5000 *Launceston Castle*, from Laira, takes the Bristol leg of the junction at Stoke Gifford. Built in 1926, this engine spent a few weeks of that same year working on the LMSR. Much has been written about the impression this engine made upon that railway, sufficient for them to build a class of engines to try and rival this one, namely the 'Royal Scots'. It has been said that the LMS actually approached the Swindon hierarchy asking for a set of drawings, perhaps this led them eventually to approach a Swindon man, Mr. Stanier, to take over at Crewe! No. 5000 was one of the first 'Castles' to be fitted with the larger 4000 gallon tender when built. The three home signals, bracketed off one post, adjacent to the 70′ dining car, shows the three routes that it is possible to take at that point. The one pulled off, which the train is taking, indicates the Bristol route via Filton Junction. The centre arm covers the route passing through the middle of the enlarged triangle, to Avonmouth via Hallen Marsh Junction and last, the outer one, is for the South Wales route through the Severn Tunnel.

Opposite page bottom:
212. A photograph which appears to be designed to confuse. This is a photograph of a down express with its train identification number proclaiming 425, which was the code for a train from Bristol! However, the train is rounding the southern leg of the junction from Stoke Gifford, which was just under 112 miles from Paddington on the Badminton route, and is approaching Bristol from the east. The fact that the train contains two LMS coaches further confuses the issue. Beyond dispute is the locomotive, No. 4908 *Broome Hall*, at this time shedded at Newton Abbot. This engine had a long association with the West of England having been sent there new in 1929. It is still coupled to a Churchward 3,500 gallon tender but eventually the whole class received larger 4,000 gallon Collett types. The train is of assorted coaches with older designs predominating. The leading vehicle is a Dean brake third, originally of diagram D25 but with the removal of its projections this is now of diagram D70. A couple of Toplights in the train have recently been repainted as their white roofs clearly show. The train might be presumed to be working from the Midlands, over the former MR route, over which the GW had running rights. The mile post indicates the miles to London as mentioned above, but the single figure '1' below this indicating a quarter of a mile extra, a half mile would have two and the three-quarter three.

214. Near the triple junction at the west end of Stoke Gifford yard is a train which, to say the least, is most interesting. It is composed entirely of non-corridor stock – not that unusual – but it is running on the wrong line which is interesting, with the signal off! It must in fact be being pushed not pulled by the tank engine and going down the centre leg of the junction towards Hallam Marsh and Avonmouth. The reason for this working is unknown but it might be a workman's train going to the aircraft factory at Filton. Another explanation might be that it is reversing down to Filton West junction from where it can come back up to Filton station, so reversing its train. The engine is one of Bath Road Shed's '55XX' class, No. 5566. It was allocated there for a number of years, although it had spells at other sheds, being at Wells, Weston-Super-Mare and Swindon. Completed in 1929 it was among the last of these lovely little engines to be built. The first coach is one of the largest class of coach constructed by the Great Western, an 8-compartment third to design C10, over 200 of which were built. Next is a vehicle not normally seen on duties such as this, a slip coach of diagram F14, followed by ex-tri-composite, now third C14. The rest are mostly a mixture of types of clerestory except the second from last which is an unidentifiable elliptically roofed composite.

215. A London engine, No. 9311, one of the rare '93XX' class, takes the South Wales route from Stoke Gifford. These engines were the last of the numerous mixed traffic 2-6-0s to appear being designed by Holcroft for Churchward. The last 20 of the class came out in 1932, after a gap of nearly 10 years (save for two being built in 1925) and as can be seen, were fitted with Collett's standard cab. No. 9311 was completed in March 1932 and when seen here was probably shedded at Old Oak Common. The second and third wagons are particularly interesting. The first of these is branded 'William Perch Ltd.' of Cardiff and Swansea, the other is 'Rigus', again of Cardiff and Swansea, but both have the same motif on the doors, a form of X. Some other wagons, behind the empty macaws, would appear to be carrying pit-props.

216. An 'up' local train approaches Stoke Gifford West Junction during the summer of 1936. Comprising a clerestory third and a 'B' set (two close-coupled brake composites), it has two Siphon G vans and an LNER perishable van added. The 'B' set was of a type found mainly in the Bristol area, all of them going there when built. On a running-in turn from Swindon Works, No. 2940 *Dorney Court* was at Bristol's Bath Road shed for some time but following this overhaul, it remained at Swindon for the rest of 1936 and all of 1937 until it returned to the Works at the end of the year, going from there to Pontypool Road early in 1938. Note that the boiler has been on a locomotive with outside steam pipes. The mark on the smokebox door isn't one normally seen, even in bright sunlight. To the right is the South Wales direct line curving around towards Patchway.

217. A beautifully clean 'Star' class No. 4019 *Knight Templar* rounds the curve from Filton Junction to Stoke Gifford with the 11.45 a.m. Bristol – Paddington express. As the identity of this train is known, some interesting points can be pointed out about the train composition. In this case, the coaches worked out from Paddington as part of the 6.30 p.m. Plymouth express. These were detached at Bristol to form this train the next day, and so on each day. We know that in the late 1920s the train was made up from the GW articulated sets as follows:- Third class triplet, Dining triplet set, First class twin; a corridor composite was added at the head on Mondays only. When in the early 1930s the articulated Third and First sets were rebuilt as individual separate vehicles, the make-up was changed to that seen in this photograph. However, the articulated dining set is still in use, but when these too were rebuilt in the mid 1930s separate vehicles were used.

218. This is the only view we have of the important junction at Patchway and unfortunately most of it is hidden by a 'down' express. The tracks turn away to the right to Bristol via Filton, those behind the train curving round to the left on the high embankment seen above the wagons is the main London to South Wales route. This was opened in 1904 and called the Badminton cut-off saving trains the longer slower route through Chippenham, Bath and Bristol, diverting from Brunel's line at Wooton Bassett. The points for the junction may be discerned under the fifth vehicle, immediately below the tall home signal. In the foreground is the scissors junction into the 'down' goods loop, mentioned previously in plate No. 66 in Volume 1, which was taken from the guards steps. The 'up' lines have moved away from the 'down' tracks, probably to ease any acuteness on the crossings. The train is, according to the index, a Brighton – Cardiff, but isn't. It is more likely to be the 7.45 a.m. Penzance – Crewe, leaving Bristol at 2.10 p.m., although there was usually LMS stock in the train. The leading vehicle, if the assumption is correct, is on a Trowbridge – Manchester working, one of five similar vans used for this service, being attached at Bristol. These five vans were allocated to this route in 1923 and were still used in 1938. This particular member is, going by vehicle painting details, one of three numbered 1082-1084. The first two carriages were attached at Newton Abbot and the restaurant car, one of the series built especially for cross-country services such as this to H38, was added at Plymouth, going through to Liverpool. No. 4096 *Highclere Castle* was to eventually achieve the second highest mileage for the class at nearly 2 million miles, or over 1100 miles a week for over 35 years for an initial cost of under £7,000! A number of interesting private owner wagons stand in the siding on the left.

Opposite page top:
219. A view from an overbridge at the western end of Patchway station early in 1936, of a north to west express climbing the last few yards to the summit of the incline from Patchway Tunnel. It would appear that some embankment repair work is being carried out adjacent to the first coach. The beautifully clean 'Star' class No. 4046 *Princess Mary* was allocated to Shrewsbury shed at this period. Constructed in 1914 it was one of the first fitted with a 4-cone ejector from new and was also originally fitted with 'I' section coupling rods, but these were replaced with the more usual rectangular section type. The tender is another of the Dean 4,000 gallon variants, this No. 1514 of the second batch constructed in 1901 on lot A51. Attached during November 1935 it remained with No. 4046 until May 1937. On the 'down' line a '3150' class 2-6-2T banking engine and tunnel brakevan are returning to either Pilning or Severn Tunnel Junction to await their next duties, the begrimed state of this engine forming a striking comparison to the 'Star'. The leading vehicles of the express are horseboxes, probably either returning from, or going to, a race meeting and were to be frequently seen in views of north to west trains. Further back is an LMS 12-wheel dining car. The train is the 10.32 a.m. Crewe – Plymouth, passing Patchway at about 2.30 p.m. The coaches are from Birkenhead, Liverpool and Manchester to either Plymouth or Kingswear. The LMS diner alternated on a daily basis with a similar GW vehicle.

Opposite page bottom:
220. With an unusual train for an express, No. 3363 *Alfred Baldwin* of the 'Bulldog' class heads two coaches up to Patchway station early in 1937. The first coach is a double ended slip of diagram F10 with its large vacuum reservoirs either side of the clerestory. This coach was one of twelve built between 1897 and 1903, however, when seen here, only three of these survived. Of these, records would seem to indicate this coach as being either 7099 or 7100 (the third survivor was 7088) with the former being the favourite. Both were built on lot 1032 in 1903 and were equipped later with through piping for Westinghouse brakes, enabling them to run over other companies lines. The roof tanks were fitted around 1910. During World War I slip coach workings ceased and afterwards, on the resumption of this system, new equipment was fitted. Some early slip coaches, however, were never re-equipped as they had been replaced by newer stock running less services.

221. Cardiff Canton shedded 'Grange' class 4-6-0 No. 6805 *Broughton Grange* heads a Cardiff – Bristol local train into Patchway station. The engine was completed in September 1936 and incorporated some parts from the withdrawn No. 4397. The leading coach in the train is a 6-wheeled saloon of diagram G20 described elsewhere. On the left can be seen a locomotive standing with a goods train in the 'down' loop, awaiting a clear road. Notice that the signal above the train has replaced the bracket signal

222. The driver waves as 'Castle' class No. 5012 *Berry Pomeroy Castle* pounds through Patchway station with an 'up' express to Paddington of over ten coaches. This engine was the last to be built with this pattern of inside cylinder cover and is fitted with a speedometer coupled to the rear driving wheel. A 'down' freight train waits in the goods loop, its brake van clear of the crossing. Note the facing point in the foreground is protected by a locking bar, and has the treadle bar in place, this preventing the point being unlocked and moved while a train was passing over it. These bars were longer than the longest wheelbased vehicle, so stopping a train from being split.

223. 'Grange' No. 6811 *Cranbourne Grange* heads a Cardiff – Bristol local away from Patchway towards Filton and the triangular junction between the original Bristol and South Wales Union Railway of 1863 and the South Wales – Bristol direct of 1903. The train is on the old route with part of the new in the background. A certain amount of recovered parts were reworked into the 'Granges', though how much is uncertain, with No. 6811 using parts from Churchward 2-6-0 No. 4344 originally built in January 1914 and withdrawn in July 1936. On the smokebox can be seen the frame for the train reporting numbers. Behind the tender, the leading coach is one of the 6-wheeled saloons built for family use in the 1890s.

224. A Bristol allocated 'Hall' passes through Patchway station with a west to north express. This is the 7.45 a.m. Penzance – Crewe (2.10 p.m. from Bristol) with a contingent of LMS coaches which alternated daily with a similar set of Great Western vehicles. The engine is No. 4949 *Packwood Hall* from Bath Road, which is still coupled to a small 3,500 gallon tender. The passenger brakevan was attached at Bristol having travelled from Trowbridge earlier and is going to Manchester. The two GW coaches were added at Newton Abbot and are working from Kingswear to Manchester. Four LMS coaches come next, the first of which is a diner, which had been added at Plymouth, all four of them travelling through to Liverpool. It will be noticed the amount of deviation needed to clear the 'down' side station buildings.

225. One of Shrewbury's allocated 'Stars' No. 4031 *Queen Mary* passes through Patchway with a train to the west. It comprises mostly LMS stock, only the last coach being of Great Western origin. The train has come from Shrewsbury via the Severn Tunnel, although the actual identity of its starting point or destination is not known, additional expresses of which this may be one were often shown only in the weekly schedules and not in the regular timetables. Completed in October 1910, No. 4031 was the first of the 'Queens' and the first built with a superheater.

226. Amidst a cloud of smoke and leaking steam from its cylinders 2-8-0 No. 2820 nears the summit at Patchway with an 'up' freight. One of Churchwards original series, No. 2820 coming from the second batch on lot 155, it entered service in December 1906. Through the years it was at many sheds, among them Pontypool Road (1921), Salisbury (1934), Swindon (1935), Aberdare (1938) and Cardiff (1948). Unusually it retained until the 1950s its original square front foot-plating, one of only three of the class recorded as doing so. This view was taken from the 'up' refuge siding which was level, the track on the far left being the 'down' line.

227. With a cloud of smoke and steam, a 2-6-0 nears the summit of the long hill at Patchway. The view is enhanced by the layers of snow and stark trees. Hauling this 'up' 'H' class freight is '63XX' class, No. 6343. The train has a variety of vehicles, from the 6-plank NE wagon at the front, to a tank wagon coming into view above the buffer stop. Next to the NE wagon are five LMS opens, most securely covered with tarpaulin sheets, and a number of private owner vehicles. These '63XXs' and their earlier variants were the maids-of-all-work, only being outclassed on the larger goods trains or heaviest expresses.

228. A begrimed 'Bulldog' begins the descent from Patchway with a South Wales-bound freight. It is leaving the 'down' goods loop which ran behind the station. The train, it will be noted, has not got the distant as it is required to stop at Filton Incline signalbox to enable the guard to pin down the wagon brakes. At this time No. 3356 *Sir Stafford* has less than a year to go, being withdrawn the following year. Built in November 1900 it was taken out of service in January 1936. It has one of those marvellous combined name and number plates and one wonders if they have survived. The leading wagons are quite clean, the first belonging to AAC Anthracite and the second Evans and Bevan with its heart shaped logos. The fifth wagon, an LMS 6-plank, looks to be full of scrap iron!

229. Barry allocated 2-8-0T No. 4261 ascends the long hill to Patchway passing near Cattybrook brickworks with an 'up' goods train. The tracks at this point are just parting for the separate bores of the tunnels through to Patchway. The line on which the train is running being somewhat lower here, easing the gradient for those trains climbing the hill. These engines were one of Churchward's standard designs, used for shorthaul work, principally in the Welsh coalfields for the short journeys to the ports. No. 4261 was built in 1917. A most interesting view, showing the tank tops and footplate detail well and also the fact that the engine is getting low on coal.

230. A 'down' 'K' class pick-up goods stands on the curve from Stoke Gifford near the junction with the Bristol to South Wales lines at Patchway, lit by a low, wintry sun. The engine is No. 5771 built during September 1929, one of the numerous '57XX' pannier tank locomotives. It was allocated to Bristol's St. Philips Marsh shed. Behind the locomotive is a GW covered goods van of diagram V23 and a former GE vehicle. Following this pair are some PO wagons, the first belonging to Sully's and the next Baldwin's. The third vehicle might also be a Sully wagon and is equipped with a single sided brake arrangement, none being visible on this nearer side.

231. One of the former ROD engines, No. 3031, descends from Patchway station with an 'H' class freight to South Wales from the West of England. The train is leaving the 'down' refuge at about 5 mph on June 30th 1933. Built by the Government's Railway Operating Department in 1917 at the North British locomotive builders Queens Park Works, it was originally numbered 3056 when purchased and put to traffic in September 1926. However, after Swindon had inspected all 100 of these engines, it was decided to keep the first 50 and condemn the second 50 when they expired. This necessitated a certain amount of renumbering to put some of the better examples into the lower numbers and vice versa, this being one of them. By this time No. 3031 had been 'Swindonised', including the fitting of the top-feed, which did not, however, disguise its original Great Central Robinson design. On the splasher can be seen the diamond works plate which would show the NBL works building number, No. 21805 and possibly the ROD number 1838. During 1933 No. 3031 was usually shedded at Exeter but from January 1934 it moved to St. Philips Marsh, Bristol. Behind are a few loco coal wagons of three differing types, diagrams N6, N4 and two N2s.

232. This is one of a series of views taken by Mr. Soole as he records 'with and for Mr. Clinker'. The subject is the double-decked Ashton Swing Bridge on a line which left the Portishead branch near Ashton Gate station and traversed the dock area. It eventually came out again down the side of Temple Meads station. The bridge was opened in November 1906 with the road section above the railway which was double-tracked. It still stands today but the cabin and structure have long since gone. Of interest are lights including a ships lantern and the signal mast from which signals were hoisted, telling the ships when to proceed. In the background a home signal protects the railway. This view was taken one evening looking to the south.

Opposite page top:
233. A panoramic view from above the western portals of the twin tunnels at Patchway. Looking west towards the Bristol Channel, an 'up' express climbs towards the tunnel, having just passed the signalbox and brickworks at Cattybrook. The train, hauled by a 'Star' No. 4060 *Princess Eugenie*, is made up mostly of elderly clerestory vehicles and toplights with a van attached at the rear. The leading coach, a composite, shows that it has been fitted with electrical equipment, the patches on the clerestory top showing where the gas lamps were originally positioned. The next carriage, a toplight, has had some of its vents removed, common practice at this time. The difference in height between the two running lines at this point can be clearly seen, also the widening gap due to the two single bore tunnels. Taken at 12.16 p.m. on July 3rd 1933, the train is a South Wales – Torquay and Paignton working. Note that the engine is blowing its whistle as it approaches the tunnel mouth. The large Collett tender was in use with No. 4060 until the 4th of November, when it was replaced by a Churchward design. It had originally been attached in May 1932, one of the earliest recipients within the 'Star' class.

Opposite page bottom:
234. A Cardiff – Bristol train passes the scene of an accident at Cattybrook, on the climb from Pilning to Patchway. The incident happened on the 'down' line, the wreckage cleared to one side across the 'up' line. New sleepers and rail have been fitted and it looks about finished but must still have a speed restriction in force over the section because the termination board is still in place. Behind it all are the chimneys of Cattybrook brickworks. The engine with its local 'B' headcode is one of the 'Saints' proper, No. 2915 *Saint Bartholomew*. Constructed in 1907 its claim to fame is that it ran the inaugural run of the *Cheltenham Flyer* in 1923. It was never fitted with outside steam pipes. During 1934, it was at Weston-Super-Mare, Bath Road and Cardiff Sheds, as well as Swindon Works. The train, a mixed rake of corridor and non-corridor carriages of various periods, typical of the era, is running on the new 'up' line, laid in 1885 on a ruling gradient of 1 in 100. The older 'down' line drops at 1 in 68 here.

237. Standing in the evening sun against an almost model background is one of Mr. Colletts little shunting engines of the '58XX' class, No. 5806. Built shortly after the first batch of '48XX' (later '14XX') this small class did not have the glamour or fame of their sisters. These engines were never auto-fitted so could not be used on push-pull duties on branch lines nor were any of them fitted with ATC apparatus. They were based upon the rebuilds of the '517' class of 0-4-2Ts so even when they were built in 1933 the basic design was over fifty-five years old. Although designed for branch and shunting duties, the '58XX' version was always less useful than the '48XX' locomotives and this led eventually to their early withdrawal. No. 5806 was from new a Bristol engine. It appeared in January 1933 and was condemned in June 1957. However, for some years prior to that it languished in the stock sheds at Swindon, along with several others, no work being available for them. It is seen here at Bristol West, standing on the relief lines opposite Pyle Hill Goods Depot.

Opposite page top:
235. One of Bristol's allocation of diesel rail cars begins the ascent from Stapleton Road with what may be the 8.30 p.m. Bristol Temple Meads – Newport, which returns from Newport at 10.12 p.m. It then went to St. Philips Marsh Shed for its servicing, ready for its first duty the following day. This car was used on working No. 3 in the Bristol Division timetables. It is possible to see quite clearly the raised seating arrangement on this side of the car, a similar raised seat above the engine was also found on the opposite side. Some of the side panelling has been removed by the shed staff to ease maintenance. New horns have been fitted externally for these cars were very quiet and for the track gangs, a danger. No. 15 was of diagram W, completed in April 1936 and had seating for 69 people plus a luggage space with double doors on either side.

Opposite page bottom:
236. Another of the AEC-built diesel rail cars climbs away from Stapleton Road station on the 'up' relief line. This is an evening working to either Cardiff or Newport, the service appearing to be well patronised. No. 8 was delivered in March 1936 and was allocated to St. Philips Marsh as the spare to DRC's Nos. 10 and 15. Some of the valancing that surrounds the bogies has been left off, similar to that above. This photograph also shows the other side, including the raised seating, with the luggage end leading. To the left is a refuse destructor but with the building of the new M32 link motorway this is now gone, as have the main lines on the far side of the railcar. These were put down in 1891 when the section from Dr. Day's Bridge Junction was quadrupled as far as Narroways Junction.

238. An 'up' freight passes through the fields of Somerset on a mild sunny spring evening. The train is near Claverham which is just to the north of Yatton. Hauling this class 'E' goods train is one of the Churchward moguls. Originally numbered 5307 and built in January 1917, it was altered and renumbered 8307 in early 1928. The modification carried out can be seen here, being the forward extension piece to the buffer beam, designed to impart more weight on the front pony truck which would transfer to the frames in an effort to reduce flange wear on twisting routes as found in South Devon and Cornwall. However, by 1944 it was re-converted back to No. 5307 due to a shortage of engines for more lightly laid lines. It was allocated to Exeter shed at this time and carries a short safety valve cover. The goods train itself is most interesting being made-up of fitted and unfitted vans, cattle trucks and micas with some open wagons towards the rear. Of the 27 recognisable vehicles, no less than 20 of these are of GW origin – not the usual mix one expects by this period. The variation of white on the 5 micas – of 3 varieties – is to be noted.

239. A 'down' Taunton express – for Minehead and Ilfracombe – hauled by a 'Castle' passes near Somerton during 1936. The reason for such a large cutting is unknown – perhaps a small yard might have been envisaged when this section of line was opened in 1906, but it allowed Mr. Soole distance to get the whole train in view. In his notes Mr. Soole makes the comment, 'Mr. F.J. Arthur of Pershore pioneered this view point and took me to it, he was a good friend!' The engine is unidentified but was one of the range Nos. 5020 to 5029 built either in 1932 or 1934. The stock virtually covers the full spectrum of GWR Corridor stock, from a Dean clerestory to the very latest Collett type. Included are a Concertina third, Collett vehicles of different designs, a Dean composite, Dreadnought dining car and a toplight brake third.

240. An interesting photograph, taken near Somerton, of what is called an 'Ocean Special'. The train is headed by the streamlined No. 6014 *King Henry VII*. It is composed of a 70′ parcels van, Super Saloon diner No. 9118 *Princess Elizabeth*, Super Saloon, Super Saloon diner No. 9117 *Princess Royal*, followed by a 3rd class diner, kitchen/1st diner and three 70′ vehicles. The Ocean Special trains ran when ships, including some of the great liners of that period, called at Plymouth, the ships often going on to Southampton, Cherbourg, or other continental ports. The train with its luxury coaches conveyed the passengers at high speed to London within a few hours of arriving in Europe. The mail was also landed at the same time and carried in a large van, some of these bearing the legend 'Ocean Mails'.

241. 'King' class 4-6-0 No. 6023 *King Edward II* passes near Somerton with an 'up' express early in 1936. The train is composed of only 8 vehicles and is probably the 'up' Torbay express. The trees show it is winter, during which the normal formation was reduced. This allowed the spare coaches to be refurbished, then layed up in the stock sheds at Swindon or Paddington, until the summer season. In this photograph the set is largely composed of 1929 'Riviera' stock apart from a 1934-built brake-composite at the rear, which is probably a strengthening vehicle. The third and fourth vehicles are not 'Rivieras' either but the slightly later diagrams of H39 and 40. *King Edward II* carries the second type of speedometer which was fitted to the 'King' class after 1933, and lasting until 1937. This is the rod-driven Jaeger system. No. 6023 was allocated to Newton Abbot throughout its life under the GW from 1930, when built, until 1949.

242. 'King' class No. 6009 *King Charles II* speeds through Foxes Wood with an 'up' Paddington train from Bristol, hiding its rolling stock under a cloud of white smoke. This particular engine was allocated throughout its existence to Old Oak Common shed. Prominent in the scene are the water troughs on both 'up' and 'down' lines. The limited clearance between the bogie and the steel trough is clearly seen. The leading coach is a converted ex-World War I ambulance vehicle, altered and fitted with a steel panelled body after its return in the early 'twenties. To the left is the quarry, showing signs of dereliction if the rusty track in the foreground is anything to go by. Of particular interest is the rock-strata rising out of the ground.

243. An effective low angle photograph of No. 4064 *Reading Abbey* of the 'Star' class in immaculate condition heading an 'up' express from Bristol towards Bath over the water troughs at Foxes Wood. These troughs are only a few miles from Bristol but were used by trains which, whilst stopping, were unable to use the water columns or by-passed the station altogether on one of the avoiding lines. No. 4064 looks as though it has just returned from Swindon Works. During its next visit to Swindon, *Reading Abbey* was rebuilt as a 'Castle' class in February 1937. The large Collett 4,000 gallon tender was attached to this locomotive in November 1935.

244. An interesting overall view of the quarry and railway at Foxes Wood on the Bristol – Bath line which was taken at 1.35 p.m. on June 17th 1933. The midday Cardiff – Brighton train approaches the beginning of the water troughs, with its board and lamp. Alongside is the end of the 'down' line's trough. The train is hauled by one of Churchwards 'Mogul' 2-6-0 engines, this one being a '63XX', which will be taken off at Westbury or Salisbury, the train going on behind a Southern engine. Probably the first two coaches will be detached also whilst the others, mixed GW and Southern vehicles, will go on to Brighton. Both of the Celerestory's are non-corridor stock. The first, a C10, is in the brown livery and the second, a 10-compartment third, C23, is in a rather grubby brown and cream. The Southern vehicles are a 4-car set of the LSW designed 'Ironclads'. Features of interest are the array of telegraph poles, the trackwork into the quarry and the clutter of stone and materials laid around. These include a point lever in the foreground, and a small tipper truck. In the background can be seen the Foxes Wood signalbox.

245. A 'down' Cornish Riviera Limited passes Westbury station behind No. 6007 *King William III* in 1938. Most likely the train has not stopped but is running through slowly, detaching two coaches as it does so, the fireman and guard watching behind intently. The Limited, as it was known, had two coaches for Weymouth at the back when it left London. As it approached Heywood Road Junction these were slipped, part of slip working No. 2, to be picked up by an engine from Westbury. They were then taken into the station as the express proceeded on its way via the cut-off route, and the coaches were added to the 12.16 p.m. train to Weymouth. The reason given for the Limited turning off the faster route and enduring the old slow line with its speed restrictions, was, according to Mr. Soole, due to the fact that the cut-off line was, 'filled up with naval ammunition after Munich' (so much for 'peace in our time'). No. 6007 was the locomotive seriously damaged two years earlier at Shrivenham and totally rebuilt, so is still quite new when seen here. The coaches are all Centenary stock with that marvellous outline, built in 1935 to the limit of the loading gauge, so much so that the doors were recessed. Westbury Middle signalbox stands in between the tracks with a carriage and wagon examiners cabin in front. In the background a couple of spare coaches stand in the yard, Westbury being allotted 1 composite, 1 brake third and 2 thirds as spares. Among the many features of interest is the signal on the left with its arms, telegraph wires and straining wires. An ATC ramp can be seen near the crossing and the yard lamp has a most unusual ladder.

Opposite page top:
246. A 3.30 p.m. Paddington – Truro train leaves Westbury station on its journey westward. This train was one of the few expresses calling into Westbury, most going round on the by-pass route, however, two or three coaches were detached from the rear for Weymouth. On certain days during the week, extra coaches were added to the formation and on a Saturday the train went to Penzance, only stopping at Truro. The engine, from Old Oak Shed, is No. 6025 *King Henry III* which still has its rod-driven Jaeger Speedometer. In the background is a '63XX' No. 6374 from Swindon with what appears to be an LMS covered carriage truck behind. The 'King' is running on the 'down' main. The 'up' main is that nearer the camera with the 'up' Salisbury between them. The signals indicate from left to right – 'up' Salisbury to goods loop, 'up' Salisbury to 'up' main and the 'up' Salisbury starter. In the foreground is the cover over the facing point locking bar equipment.

Opposite page bottom:
247. No. 4077 *Chepstow Castle* moves out of Westbury station to continue its journey westward with the 3.30 p.m. Paddington – Truro. It leaves behind a couple of coaches which will be attached to the 5.18 p.m. Westbury – Weymouth train. Further portions were detached at Newton Abbot, for Kingswear, and the dining car and a few others at Plymouth. Only the front four coaches reached Truro and these were then forwarded to Penzance. No. 4077's home shed is Newton Abbot so it will come off there, along with the (now) last three coaches which will go on to Kingswear. A Penzance locomotive will probably replace the 'Castle. This was the fifth of the class to be built, in February 1924, and was allocated to Paddington (Old Oak Common) when new, being at Laira ten years later. Another engine was named *Chepstow Castle* until May 1923, the plates being removed to avoid confusion about the classes. This was a 'Duke' class 4-4-0, No. 3282 of 1899, which then was nameless until withdrawal in 1937. To the left are some spare carriages and in front of the station's island platform are some fine signals.

248. An unusual train but in view of the times not unexpected. A train of military personnel departs from Westbury station to, Mr Soole records, Wells. It will presumably use the main line to Witham then take the East Somerset line. It is quite possible the train has arrived from Salisbury, the soldiers coming from Salisbury Plain. Both of the engines are of the '4575' series of the '45XX' class with No. 4595 leading and the other, No. 5549, the train engine. Both are from Westbury shed and are from the batches built in the late 1920s. No. 4595 has some patches on the tank side and has the normal cab-filled rear sand box, fitted to most of the class, while No. 5549 has an externally filled variety found only on later engines. The train is of Southern Railway stock, mostly it would appear, of ex-LSWR origin, the set being No. 326, 826 or 926. The leading vehicle is to LSW drawing No. 1568, to which has been added a pressed-steel look-out by the Southern. From what can be seen 10 of the 12 coaches are 54'/56' corridor stock built in the early 1900s. A number of passengers are very youthful and what appears to be some horse-play is going on towards the rear. Standing in siding No. 1 is a freight train headed by either a 'Hall' or a 'Saint'. On the far side stands some wagons of interest, namely an ex MR motor car van of diagram D833 and a 5-plank wagon with extra rails for carrying coke belonging to Whitwell, Cole & Co., and numbered 601. Just visible between the smoke and the top of the train is an ironworks, long since demolished. The station may be seen in the distance.

249. An 'up' express takes the Westbury route from Fairwood Junction, the overbridge seen in the background being that visible on the extreme right of the following photograph. The identity of both the train and the gentleman in the distance, who appears on several views in the collection, is unknown. Hauled by 'Castle' class No. 4076 *Carmarthen Castle*, one of the first built, the coaching stock is mostly that usually associated with the South Wales routes. These are the Concertina vehicles, easily distinguishable by their many recessed doors. The fourth coach, however, was one not used in Wales, a Dreadnought dining car of 1904. All of the identifiable vehicles are of 70' length. The 'Castle', completed in February 1924, ended its days with an unusually low mileage, indeed the lowest of the first batch. It was recorded as being at Landore early in 1935 and at Carmarthen itself later, but it moved to Exeter via Swindon Works, remaining there for the next few years before moving on to Newton Abbot. When seen here early in 1936 it was allocated to Exeter.

250. The winter sun throws the shadow of this 'up' express onto the embankment side, the train recorded as the 'up' Limited. The scene is the new cut-off line recently opened by-passing the Junctions and station with its 30 m.p.h. speed restriction at Westbury. These cut-offs were laid during the early 'thirties in a government sponsored effort to relieve the unemployment problems with worthwhile tasks. One can see the beautifully neat ballast and cutting with new fencing. The engine is none other than the Great Western's impressive masterpiece No. 6000 *King George V*. This engine ran over 1,900,000 miles in 35 years and was a great favourite on specials and attending displays. The leading three coaches are some of those specially built for the GWR's centenary in 1935, the previous year, built to the maximum width and incorporating some new and unusual design concepts. Further back may be seen the massive bulk of one of Churchward's equally innovative designs of 30 years earlier, a Dreadnought dining car, so named after the Royal Navy's mighty battleship, the behemoth of the age!

251. A massive train of at least fourteen coaches takes the Westbury avoiding line. Hauled by a 'King', the train is an 'up' Torbay with seven extra coaches, all of which are thirds. No. 6025 *King Henry III* of Old Oak Common has just taken water from the Fairwood troughs a short distance back and the water is still running from the overflow and splashing off the tender back. The leading coach has had a right drenching! One hopes the coach end board was in place over the corridor connection, if not the interior could be flooded – not an unknown occurrence. The size of the train suggests that this might be a summer Saturday express, the normal daily train formation being enlarged to meet the demands of the Traffic Department.

252. What looks to be the 'down' Torbay Limited approaches Fairwood Junction during the summer of 1937. The train is running on the new by-pass section alongside the old route through Westbury. The engine is heading home to Newton Abbot and is No. 6018 *King Henry VI*. This was the engine used during the 1948 locomotive exchanges, but because of its size it was restricted to working over LNER metals from Kings Cross to Leeds. Behind are the eight coaches which make up the Torbay express including an H40 and H39 dining car set. The seventh coach only ran until October, being dispensed with during the winter months to be brought out again in May. Added to the rear are three coaches for Penzance which were removed at Exeter and forwarded on a 'down' Wolverhampton train.

253. This is thought to be a 'down' Weymouth express hauled by No. 6028 *King George VI*, which was named *King Henry II* until the accession of the new King, the engine being renamed in January 1937. The train is approaching Fairwood Junction and is passing under the GW line from Westbury to Salisbury on the Westbury cut-off. Alongside the overbridge parapet may be seen the Westbury White Horse, not to be confused with the one at Uffington near Swindon. The White Horse was cut into the chalk hill on Bratton Down during the 18th Century on the site of an earlier horse which was said to have commemorated the victory at the Battle of Ethandun by King Alfred over the Danes in 878AD.

254. The Cornish Riviera Express speeds along the Westbury by-pass line. Mr. Soole records this early 1936 photograph as the 'down' 'Limited' but it is actually the 'up' train seen here. The leading two coaches, brake composites, were normally detached from the rear on the 'down' journey for various destinations, four in total during the summer. These were collected on the return trip at the head of the train so as to be correctly marshalled for the following days 'down' run again. The vehicles are all of the 1935 centenary stock specially built for the Limited. Note how quickly the roofs have discoloured from the original white. The train engine, itself looking rather scruffy, is the streamlined 'King' No. 6014 *King Henry VII* with some of the airflow smoothing panels removed. These were fitted early in 1935 to this engine and a 'Castle' to assess the reduction in resistance that such panels may make. They were not very successful or practical from a maintenance point of view and were gradually taken off.

255. Water streams from the tender as No. 2927 *Saint Patrick* leaves the troughs at Fairwood Junction. The train is an 'up' express from the Torbay area and as the engine is allocated to Swindon, presumably the train will go into Westbury and run via Trowbridge and Chippenham to that destination. The smokebox on the boiler in the photograph has had outside steam pipes fitted to it when on another engine, No. 2927 not being so altered until July 1945. The tender, a Churchward 3,500 gallon type, was to remain with this engine until June 1939. The coach leading is a Collett brake third with one of the massive Dreadnought thirds behind it. The contrast in styles, height, width and waist levels is most apparent, the other major railway companies not having the noticeable disparity in the paintwork because of their one colour paint schemes.

256. A 'King' passes Fairwood Junction with an 'up' express and takes the cut-off line instead of going through Westbury, to where the lines to the right lead. The 'down' line has a speed restriction in force, the termination of which is marked by the sign on the left. No. 6023 *King Edward II* still has its shaft driven speedometer at this time, possibly the last engine to carry it, the standard type being fitted to most by 1937. This engine is not recorded as being fitted with the Jaeger instrument. The bogie is a one-off and has a slotted front stretcher beam. This was also noted on several of the class through the years.

257. An 'up' express thunders over the water troughs at Fairwood Junction, spray flying as tons of water are taken aboard the tender. The engine is No. 6009 *King Charles II* from Old Oak Common shed. In fact this engine was never anywhere else, spending its entire career of over 34 years at the one shed. This 'up' train started from Plymouth and is the second part. It is largely comprised of 70′ vehicles at the front and there are around fourteen coaches in the train in total. The water troughs are fed from two tanks, one each for the 'up' and 'down' lines. The area around the tracks has been paved with large stones in an attempt to prevent the ballast being washed away, the down-wash from an engine at speed being quite considerable.

258. A 'down' West of England express runs along the Westbury avoiding line on a misty morning behind No. 6028 *King George VI*. It is passing under the Westbury to Salisbury line which skirts the edge of Salisbury Plain. This was an important link line, over which many inter-company trains ran between the north and midlands to the channel ports. Tragically No. 6028 crashed at Norton Fitzwarren in 1940 in one of the worst accidents ever on the Great Western. It is still fitted here with a Jaeger speedometer arrangement. Most of the coaches discernible behind the engine are third class vehicles from different periods, some of which are 70′ in length. The train is the second part of what may be the 'down' Torbay express.

259. With Twyford signalbox and station visible in the background an 'up' express speed towards the capital. The train is a short one but none the less is of great interest. The view would have been taken during the summer of 193? Some years earlier, the GWR equipped No. 4085 *Berkeley Castle* with an experimental fire iron tunnel which is seen here still in place. It certainly does not have the neatness of the later pattern. As far as can be ascertained, this is the first time a photograph of this feature has been published and an enlargement is included showing it in more detail. Unfortunately No. 4085 has other claim to fame (if one can call it that), is that this is the locomotive which knocked down and killed G.J. Churchward one foggy morning in December 1933, when working a 'down' South Wales express. This train is of interest and might well be an 'up' train from Wales. The leading van, to diagram K41 is painted in the all over brown livery introduced a couple of years earlier. After this is, with the exception of the diner, a rake of four 70′ coaches, two Toplight and two Concertina brake thirds. The diner, the third vehicle, is one of the small 57′ Toplight style coaches, six of which were built in 1908, diagram H16. The track in the foreground is a recently laid section of concrete sleepered track work, laid to assess its potential!

260. A light express rushes eastward towards Paddington having passed through Twyford and approaching Ruscombe. The train is hauled by 'Castle' No. 5022 *Wigmore Castle* from Old Oak Common. Completed in August 1932, this was the last 'Castle' built with the front lampbracket on the smokebox top, after this new engines had the bracket attached to the door and most of the earlier locomotives were altered to suit. The coaches, with the exception of the second vehicle, a buffet car, are all Toplights, of both steel and wooden bodied varieties. Of note in this photograph are the pair of double-sided distant signals situated outside of the running lines with their linking indicator and telegraph wires. Note that each had an independent ladder.

261. One of the most famous members of the 'Castle' class approaches Maidenhead station with an 'up' express. No. 4074 *Caldicot Castle* was the second engine of the class and a noted 'flyer'. The first dynamometer tests with the 'Castles' were performed using this engine and proved outstanding. During the 1925 exchanges it also excelled when running against the LNER Pacifics. Built in 1923, some alterations have been made to the engine since then, but none detract from its fine lines. The train of mixed types includes a 70' restaurant car which has been refurbished. The first coach is a wooden bodied Toplight brake third but it is possible to see that a certain amount of the bodywork has been covered with metal sheeting where body rot has been found – the curse of the wooden stock. In the foreground is a siding laid in a light gauge flat-bottom rail of short length. This siding was used for storing stock but only a small, light engine would be allowed to run on it. Notice the signals set away from the running lines for better visibility.

262. As a 'down' express passes Twyford (east) signalbox in the distance, an 'up' Cheltenham train speeds towards London. This is probably the 2.40 p.m. due into Paddington at 5.00 p.m. An extra coach has been added, this, the third from the rear, identifiable by having no roof label board. Where this was attached is not known. The five coaches in front of it all started from Cheltenham but the dining car following was not added until Gloucester. At the back is a brake composite which is working from Hereford, this also being put on at Gloucester. The engine is only just over a year old, being built in 1936 as No. 5043 *Barbury Castle* but is very soon to be renamed on September 10th as *Earl of Mount Edgcumbe*. In the foreground is a milepost indicating 30½ miles to Paddington.

263. The 'up' Bristolian thunders past a westbound freight as it trundles along the 'down' relief between Twyford and Ruscombe. The partially streamlined 'King' No. 6014 *King Henry VII* returns to London, its home shed, after travelling out on a morning train. Some of the panels fitted in March of the previous year have already gone, to ease maintenance and prevent overheating. Other bits gradually followed, the domed nose sometime during World War II. When the locomotive was condemned in 1962 only the V shaped cab front remained. One curious after effect was when the nose was eventually taken off, the train reporting boards (which had to be fitted to the footplate instead of the smokebox door) remained there. The train is of very modern stock, as one might expect, although the buffet car just appearing behind the brakevan is a few years older.

264. A long freight train rattles into Maidenhead, crossing the High Wycombe line, as it heads east, cleared to run through the station on the 'up' relief. It is passing a line of coaches and vans standing on the siding seen in a previous view, to the left across the main line. The '43XX' class were derived from the large Prairie 2-6-2Ts, and designed for Churchward by Holcroft after his visit to America. They were very capable engines and were only eclipsed by the introduction of the 'Hall' class, but continued to provide the GWR with an all round ability. They were at home on a light express train or a humble freight. The regulation for the provision of two wagons between the engine and any dangerous load is complied with here by the use of two 7-plank opens before the tank wagons. The building to the right is a shunters cabin and is covered with enamel notices. One even advertising the West Sussex Gazette (in Berkshire!). Behind the tank wagons is Maidenhead Middle signalbox.

265. With the Thames in the background, a 'Hall' has a less glamorous task than usual, hauling a London-bound 'H' class freight. It is running on the 'up' relief towards Pangbourne on a lovely, sunny summers day in 1934. No. 4969 *Shrugborough Hall* is homeward-bound to Old Oak Common. These locomotives were the first purely mixed-traffic engines, equally at home on freight, as we see here, or heavy expresses. They were constructed in large numbers over a period of some 22 years (disregarding the prototype, *Saint Martin*, of 1924) and the class consisted of over 300 engines. They eventually spread through the whole of the Great Western's system and could be found at most large sheds and on any 'red' route. The 'Halls' took over many duties from the now ageing '43XX' series on tasks that the smaller locomotives were being found wanting. Behind the 4,000 gallon tender, which has replaced the earlier and smaller 3,500 gallon type, is a miscellaneous collection of wagons and vans. The first vehicle is one of the ubiquitous GW iron minks. Following on are an LMS steel-end van, a GW 'open C' and a 'mite', (the small wagon with the single bolster) in all over 50 vehicles.

266. *Above:* A 'Hall' class locomotive storms past Filton Incline signalbox with an 'up' freight under an 'H' headcode. This code allowed the train to proceed at a maximum of 35 m.p.h. At this point the train is running on the 'up' relief line, the 'up' and 'down' main lines being those nearest the camera. When the train reaches Filton Junction, it can either crossover to the London lines or carry straight on to South Wales. On the former it would be an 'up' train, on the latter, a 'down' train – a rather confusing situation. The engine is 4-6-0 No. 5910 *Park Hall* and the stock a mixture of mainly vans with a high proportion of GWR types.

267. *Left:* A glimpse inside of a signalbox of the day, this one being Filton Incline. Look at the paraphenalia, the bells and instruments. In the diagram above the shelf can be seen part of the trackplan looking downhill towards Bristol, taking in Horefield station. It would seem the new frame enclosing this plan has been placed over the earlier copy, superseded in 1933 by the new track layout, and in fact tied on with a bit of rope! Two gaps of 3 levers each have been left in the lever frame, for future additions, the frame being capable of 35 levers. Among the instruments on the shelf, those with the dials are train describers and the other large item is the permissive block instrument with its block bell next to it. Look at the wiring under the shelf, at least someone has had the sense to tag a few of the wires with cardboard labels.

270. An 'up' freight nears Pilning station on its climb away from the Severn Tunnel. Hauled by a '28XX' and with a pilot engine, a member of the '3150' class, the train will come to a stand at the station. The pilot will draw forward into a siding and the train will move ahead, permitting the pilot to attach itself to the rear to bank the freight up to Patchway. There it will drop off, taking with it one of the specially enclosed tunnel brakevans which were always attached to the rear. They will then either stay at Patchway or return to Pilning to await further duties. This pilot engine has the target number 4 on its front. The bracket signal to the right has a most unusual post, perhaps a metal one. Notice too the roof of the car on the bridge. Through the bridges may be seen the hill under which is Ableton Lane Tunnel.

Previous page top:
268. A north to west express leaves the east portal of the Severn Tunnel wreathed in smoke as it tackles the continuing steady climb and is about to enter the short Ableton Lane Tunnel. Above the hill can be just discerned one of the pumping stations for 'The Hole'. These daily pumped out millions of gallons so preventing the tunnel flooding. This particular locomotive was used regularly on this turn and may be seen in several photographs. No. 4999 *Gopsal Hall* was completed in 1931 and passed between several sheds, but is almost certainly either from Shrewsbury or Laira when seen here. In fact it was a Laira engine by 1938. The train includes a restaurant car of diagram H38, this alternated daily with a similar LMS vehicle. The horsebox (this working usually seems to have one) is an ex-LNWR D436 and there is, what looks to be, a GW example at the rear. This was one of a number of photographs taken in March 1936 containing views of horseboxes. We know that one of them was credited with being a return working from the Grand National at Aintree, Liverpool. The National was not the social event in those days it is today, indeed it was run on a Friday. In 1936 the race was held on the 27th March and was won by Reynoldstown for the second consecutive year.

Previous page bottom:
269. Viewed approaching Pilning High Level station early in 1936, an 'up' South Wales express climbs away from the undersea tunnel crossing of the Severn, a constant climb for some 8¼ miles to Patchway, the summit. This Old Oak allocated engine, No. 5004 *Llanstephan Castle*, has nine vehicles behind, eight coaches and a van, most of which, van included, are 70' stock. The train has two dining cars at the front, the first one of the two Toplight brake thirds altered to provide a small buffet and numbered 2355 or 2365. They were reconverted in 1936, so may just be still used for this purpose although they are noted as being returned to ordinary traffic during 1934. The next diner is an H13 still with its original windows. Later in the 1930s most of these coaches were substantially altered under another government sponsored scheme to help create employment.

271. A north to west express runs through the north Somerset countryside near Nailsea with No. 5008 *Raglan Castle*. On the right is Chevley Court with an orchard beyond. In the distance behind the very tall distant signal (for easier viewing over the bridge from which the photograph was taken) is Nailsea station. The train contains eight coaches, four GW and four LMS, which formed the 1.10 p.m. Crewe – Plymouth where it arrived at shortly after 9.00 p.m. The leading vehicle, a GW Toplight brake composite is on a Birkenhead – Plymouth working. The four LMS coaches, a brake third of LNW D313 with a cove roof and two LNW toplights, a composite of D131 and brake third to D306, are followed by what looks to be an LMS 12-wheel diner, probably diagram I811, are all working alternatively with GW stock on the Liverpool – Plymouth portion. Next are three GW coaches, working from Manchester, the first to Plymouth and the last two to Kingswear.

272. The 12.15 p.m. Penzance – Crewe leaves the four-track section north of Yatton near Claverham in Somerset. Cows graze peacefully taking no notice of No. 6016 *King Edward V* from Laira shed (its home for over 24 years) as it speeds by. The engine is in sparkling condition as it heads towards Bristol where it will be replaced. Behind the engine is a TPO van of diagram L22. This too will come off at Bristol when it arrives at 7.00 p.m. to return to Plymouth early the next morning. The leading coach which, like the TPO and the locomotive, was attached at Plymouth and will also be detached at Bristol. The dog kennel-like box, neatly set into the ash adjacent to mile post 128 3/4, is a ballast-bin.

273. *Above:* The crew of an 'Aberdare' have both taken a rest to watch Mr. Soole taking this picture, as their train ambles through the countryside heading north-east towards Bristol near Long Ashton at about 20 m.p.h. No. 2675 was built in November 1902 but when seen here on April 11th 1933 it had about two years left before withdrawal, during September 1935. It ended its days working from Bristol's St. Philips Marsh shed. The train itself contains a mixture of wagons and vans, including a Macaw loaded with logs and a number of presumably empty PO wagons at the front. Classified as a 'K' in the head lamp signals listings or an ordinary goods, stopping at intermediate stations, generally known as a pick-up goods. When the photograph was taken the old headcodes of 1926 or earlier were still in use, but later, in August 1936, new head-codes were introduced. These may cause some confusion when looking at similar trains after that date which shows a different headlamp grouping.

274. *Left:* Taken a couple of years earlier than plate No. 272. A 'Bulldog' No. 3446 *Goldfinch*, hurries its Bristol-bound local past Claverham signalbox at the end of the 1½ mile section of four tracks north of Yatton. These were 'up' and 'down' goods running loops, put into operation in April 1925, and 'up' and 'down' main lines. Completed in November 1909, No. 3446 looks in fine condition. A Bath Road allocated engine when seen here, it spent over two months – April and May of 1934 – in Swindon Works, so we can presume this view shows it shortly afterwards. Immediately behind the 3,500 gallon tender is a Siphon G of the inside-framed variety. At the rear of the train, behind the last coach, appears to be a water tank wagon, which was painted white. Note the well-groomed appearance of the trackwork and edges, also the point rodding running back towards the signalbox.

275. A freight train emerges from the Severn Tunnel into daylight and fresh air. The driver of the second locomotive looks to be taking a well-earned breather as the smoke continues to pour out of the tunnel entrance. It must be remembered there are still two guards in their vans in the tunnel as yet. One only has to look at the condition of the front engine which spent all of its duties shuttling backwards and forwards through 'the Hole', as the enginemen called it, to appreciate the conditions. On the leading locomotive, a '3150' class 2-6-2T, can be seen its target or duty number, in this instance No. 1, which indicates to the signalmen the train and its destination and whether it would continue after Pilning banking the '28XX' up the hill to Patchway. The leading wagons are for coke, having extra boards fitted to the sides to get more in, as coke is lighter than coal. The building in the background is Severn Tunnel East signalbox with the unusual sighting board above it for a signal up the hill, behind Mr. Soole.

276. A stopping or pick-up goods train drops down towards Bristol from Filton late one summer evening. The train is running on the 'down' main, unusually for a train which has presumably come from South Wales. Engine No. 5260 has not many weeks left before withdrawal, in mid 1935. It was to reappear in October of that year from Swindon rebuilt as a 2-8-2T No. 7225, after having the frames at the rear extended and a pony truck added. This increased the water and coal capacity, comparable in fact to a small tender, making an extremely useful engine for medium distance freights and the like. No. 5260 was withdrawn from Newport Pill Shed, the rebuilt engine going to Llanelly. A replacement No. 5260 was built at Swindon in February 1940. Two LMS steel ended vans are at the front, similar in design but one having roof vents. Behind these is a tar tank wagon with a pair of Baldwin 7-planks next. Following these is an MR designed van, a heavily tarpaulined vehicle and an NE wagon, after which is a GW Macaw J, then a totally unidentifiable 6-wheeled wagon carrying what looks like a bush! The late evening sun throws the shadow of the signalbox across the relief lines.

277. An unidentified member of the '53XX' class climbs away from Bristol, passing Narroways Hill Junction with what is reputed to be a Brighton-Cardiff train. Whilst it was not unusual to see this class with express headcodes, views of them with train reporting numbers as well, are rare. It is probable that it is deputising for a failed engine. The train reporting number is somewhat confusing as this was of a sequence allocated to trains starting from either Wolverhampton or Birmingham, so this might in fact be a return working to the Midlands running via the Midland line from Westerleigh to Standish Junctions. The coaching stock appears to be all of GW origin, at least as far as the Clerestory coach. Behind the train, through the footbridge, can be seen the junction and the Stapleton Road area of Lower Easton.

278. A '4575' class tank engine swings off the 'down' main line onto the branch line to Portishead with a Sunday local passenger train on July 23rd 1933. The rebuilding of Parson Street Tunnel, over which passes the main A38, is under way. On the extreme right is a contractors engine and behind it, on a lightly laid track, are some wagons and a steam crane. It is through this that the new lines will be laid making this a 4-track section. A photograph looking the other way can be seen in Volume 1, plate 1. All the rebuilding which went on in Bristol at this period was, among other things, designed to speed traffic through the city with quadruple tracks from South Liberty Junction through to Filton Junction. To be noted is the temporary footbridge over the railway, point rodding, railwayman's access from street level and power cables on hangers.

Appendix 1

In the first volume we laid out the reference for the carriage and freight stock identification. Obviously what was written then holds good here, so we shall dispense with that information and refer the reader to it. An up-dated list of the carriages which appear in this work follows, in a similar order to that used previously.

The restaurant cars are listed seperately. This is because many of these, whilst built to the style current at that date, do not fit into the standard in which we would place them, particularly some of the earlier designs. Many of these were one-off or small batches or even short term conversions from ordinary coaches, to be used on certain trains regardless of the rest of the stock. Examples appear in this book, in particular the use of the articulated set and buffet cars on particular services.

Some explanation about diagrams is required. When the system was put into practice in the early 1900s, the diagrams were issued commencing from the oldest through to what was then the newest stock. At the time this was taking place, the Great Western also took the opportunity to abandon the then second class accommodation – although a letter, 'B', was issued but never used. From the time of the implementation of the scheme, all subsequent designs were allotted the next number in sequence. However, most will see from the following lists that there were some anomalies within the diagram series, due primarily to rebuilding or alteration within the original design or because of the downgrading of older vehicles.

A further cause of confusion was the rebuilding in the early 'twenties of a large number of vehicles which had been sold to the government during the First World War. These were re-purchased and taken to Swindon. They had been used either in ambulance trains or as accommodation for staff. Some of these coaches needed only to be refurbished, but many were in poor condition and required totally rebuilding. Some of them retained their original underframes while others had even these renewed. A large number of the passenger coaches were fitted with steel panelling during the rebuilding, with some of the unnecessary fitments, such as the toplights, being plated over. Within the general scheme most of these vehicles were given later diagrams though were still identified by their underframe designs. The rebuilding took several years, so spreading themselves amongst the newly designed and built stock, their diagrams reflecting this time span.

Prior to the appointment of William Dean as Locomotive, Carriage & Wagon Superintendent in 1877, the coaching stock of the Great Western Railway was in a decrepit state due to the need to provide both standard and Broad Gauge vehicles in a poor financial climate. Much of the stock was quite old and included some from absorbed lines swallowed up by the expanding GWR. Dean's early work was to provide new standard gauge vehicles to meet the requirements of the expansion of that gauge due to the taking over of others and the conversion of former Broad Gauge routes. There was also the need to provide new coaches for the Broad Gauge itself, although much of the later stock was convertible.

The Dean coaches were typically Victorian, ranging from the basic, through to the opulent. Following the introduction of the first corridor train in the early 1890s, large numbers of gangwayed vehicles were built during the next ten years, the same period also seeing the introduction of the Great Western's first electrically lit stock and dining cars.

Churchward's coaches, like his engines, were different. While still building the last of the clerestory designs, he introduced the Dreadnought dining car, which were the first elliptical roofed vehicles. The clerestory was an expensive and weak structure. Following the massive Dreadnoughts came the Concertinas and the Toplights, many of the latter being similar to their clerestory roofed predecessors in both design and layout but with the elliptical roof. By the end of his tenure, Churchward had gone on to introduce electrical equipment into all stock and to fit steel panelling in place of the previous wooden panels (although these were painted to match the earlier styles).

Collett's policy with both locomotives and carriages, was to follow Churchward's principles, although he did experiment with both articulation and buck-eye couplings, and introduced the bow-ended stock. It wasn't until the 1929 ' Riviera' designs that he produced anything different, but from then, for the next six years or so, we see the introduction of the finest carriage stock to be built by the Great Western Railway. In 1930, Collett designed the magnificent 'Super Saloons', probably the peak of Swindon-built vehicles, followed four years later by the equally impressive 'Centenary' stock which were the best available to the general public. The range of standard vehicles designed at this time were very modern and not out of place twenty years later. From 1929 many inventive schemes were tried, among them metal framing (even until after the Second World War, coaches were still steel panelled on wooden frames), open stock and buffet cars. Strangely, Collett still used different lengths for different stock (in 1931-2, he used three separate lengths and two widths in various combinations) and he reverted to a flat-end profile. Collett's period might be looked upon as being in two parts, 1922 to 1929 and from 1929 onward.

Dean

Various lengths, though normally 8′6″ wide, with a flat 3-arc roof or differing forms of clerestory roof.

non-clerestory:
> G20, K15, K26/29, K30.

clerestory non-gangwayed:
> C3, C4, C10, C14, C22, C23, D21, D24, E105, F10, K12.

clerestory, gangwayed:
> A7, C16, C17, D25+, D30, D31, D70, D103, E66+, E69+, E73, G33.

Churchward

Dreadnought:
> C24

Concertina:
> C27, D43, E79, E80, F13.

Toplight
Bars I:
> Bar truss underframe, horizontal eave panels and single toplight above end corridor windows.
> 56′: C30, D46, E82, E85, E87.
> 57′: C31, C49, D44, D45, D47, D80, E83, E88.
> 70′: C29, E84.

Bars II:
> Bar truss underframe, panels alongside windows go to cantrail and double toplights above end corridor windows.
> 57′: C31, C32, D47, D52, E88, E95, F20.
> 70′: C29, D51, E93.

Multibar:
> Twin rod truss underframe, same body as Bars II, later steel panelled.
> 57′: A13, C31, C32, D47+, D56, D88, E98, E103.
> 70′: C29, C33, D51, D57, D69, E99, E102, E104.

Angle truss:
Angle truss underframe and steel panelled bodies.
57': C32, D56, D80, D88.
70': C38, D57, D69, E99, E102, E104.
Non-gangwayed:
F14.

Collett

1922 Gangwayed:
57' x 8'6": E113.
57' x 9': E114, E115/8.
70' x 9': C44+, D82/4, D83/90, E109/11, E110/12.
1923/24 Gangwayed:
58' x 9': C54, D94, E127, E128.
1925/26 Gangwayed:
58' x 9': D95.
57' x 9': E132.
1928 Gangwayed:
58' x 9': C58, D104.
1929 Gangwayed:
61' x 9'5¾": C59, D105, D106, D108, E137, E138.
61' x 9': C60, D107, E139.
1930 Gangwayed:
61' x 9'3": C62, E143.
61' x 9'7": G60.
1931/32 Gangwayed:
61' x 9'3": C64, D115.
60' x 9'3": C65.
57' x 9': D116, E146.
1933 Gangwayed:
57' x 9': D118.

1934 Gangwayed:
57' x 9' C67, E148.
61' x 9'7": C69, D120, E149, E150.
1935 Gangwayed:
61' x 9': C70, D121.
58' x 9': E151.
1936/38 Gangwayed:
61' x 9': C73, C77, D124, E152, D127.
57' x 9': A18 (ex-articulated).
58' x 9': E154.
60' x 9': A20, C74, E155, E158.
Non-gangwayed:
C43, C56, C61/3, C66, C75, D117, E147.
'B' sets. (Close-coupled, non-gangwayed brake composites).
E116, E140, E145.

Restaurant and Dining cars
68' – 71': H8/11, H13/14, H15, H19, H24, H26+.
56'/57': H16, H17/18, H25/33, H41.
46'/50': H30-H31-H32 articulated set.
60'/61': H38, H39, H40, H43, H44, H45, H46, H52, H54.

Passenger Brake Vans & Brown vehicles
Dean:
K12, K15, K26/29, K30, N8, O4.
Churchward:
K22, M10, N14, O11.
Collett:
K40, K41, L22, N15, N16, O22, O33.

No. 4093 *Dunster Castle* passes the brickworks near Bristol West Depot. Apart from a network of sidings, there was also the junction for the Portishead line, which ran along the south side of the Avon Gorge. The full name of the brickworks was 'The South Liberty Brick and Tile Works'. The footbridge gives access to it from Bedminster Down. *Dunster Castle* from Newton Abbot at this time, was notable as the first 'Castle' to have straight frames. Before this, the frames were 'joggled' above the bogie. From this engine onwards they were straight, with a 'dishing' on the lower edge above the front bogie wheels for sideplay clearance. The leading vehicle is one of Churchward's massive 68' 'Dreadnought' third class coaches, of diagram C24. This is one of the series built by Birmingham C&W, identifiable by the wider door recesses. These carriages were not popular with travellers because they had access to the compartments only from the corridor. The compartments were also staggered, four to one side, five the other, with a vestibule in the centre for access and changeover. It has been fitted with the 9' modern bogies. Just under the footbridge is a 70' restaurant car from the second series to diagram H15, these not having the recessed double doors of their sisters although they were all built on the same lot (No. 1131) and to the same diagram.

Train Formations

One of the points overlooked last time was to explain in the train formation lists the reason for the + sign after certain diagrams of coaches. This is where we find difficulty differentiating between the various similar designs, which were externally identical to others but had an internal or minor alteration. Swindon, on such occasions, issued another diagram. In these instances, we have shown the first of the possible diagrams.

Intro. No. 100 A1 *Lloyds* built 5/07, rebuilt 4/25, withdrawn 3/50. G33, D124, –.

135. No. 2938 *Corsham Court* built 12/11, withdrawn 8/52. H8/11, H24, –.

136. No. 3407 *Madras* built 4/04, withdrawn 12/49. W–, C54+, C60, D45, C54+, –, D–.

137. No. 2340 built 6/84, withdrawn 6/54. E148, –.

138. No. 6105 built 5/31, withdrawn 3/60. D21, C43, C56/61, –.

139. No. 53XX class.

140. No. 5255 built 12/25, withdrawn 9/35. N24, N2, N24, –.

141. No. 4073 *Caerphilly Castle* built 8/23, withdrawn 5/60 (preserved). E80, H15, E109/11, –.

142. No. 4056 *Princess Margaret* built 7/14, withdrawn 10/57. K12, D118, C67, E127+, E148, –.

143. No. 4055 *Princess Sophia* built 7/14, withdrawn 2/51. D116, E137, C–, D–, –.

144. No. 4033 *Queen Victoria* built 11/10, withdrawn 6/51. D105, C54+, C54+, H32-H31-H30, E127/32, E79, D45+.

145. No. 6000 *King George V* built 6/27, withdrawn 12/62.

146. No. 5022 *Wigmore Castle* built 8/32, withdrawn 12/63. D95 No. 4943, E127+.

147. No. 5158 built 3/30, withdrawn 4/61. D95 No. 4943, E127+.

148. No. 5004 *Llanstephan Castle* built 6/27, withdrawn 4/62. C38, H17/18, H13/14, E127+, C44+, D43, –.

149. No. 4061 *Glastonbury Abbey* built 5/22, withdrawn 3/57. SR (ex-LSWR) Ironclad stock, –.

150. No. 5032 *Usk Castle* built 5/34, withdrawn 9/62. W–, E82, C54+, D–, C17, –, –, LMS, LMS, –.

151. No. 4034 *Queen Adelaide* built 11/10, withdrawn 9/52. D108, H24, E88, C67, –.

152. No. 5016 *Montgomery Castle* built 7/32, withdrawn 9/62. LMS stock –.

153. No. 2821 built 1/07, withdrawn 9/60. B & C, –.

154. No. 4301 built 6/11, withdrawn 8/36. Blaenavon, Blaenavon, –.

155. No. 5007 *Rougemont Castle* built 6/27, withdrawn 9/62. D47 No. 2379, E84, H13/14, –.

156. No. 6027 *King Richard I* built 7/30, withdrawn 9/62. D121, C70, E151, H41, A20, E151, D121.

157. No. 4083 *Abbotsbury Castle* built 5/25, withdrawn 1/62. D121, C77, E154, H8/11, C77, D121, C77, E–, –.

158. No. 4045 *Prince John* built 6/13, withdrawn 11/50. SR (ex-LSWR) set No. 436 – Bk. third, first,, third, bk. third; Bulleid compo., Bulleid third.

159. No. 4068 *Llanthony Abbey* built 1/23, withdrawn 11/38 (rebuilt). LMS (ex. Midland Rly). PBV No. 32828, E87, D95, E127+, D115, LMS diner D1243, E.–, D.–, –.

160. No. 4068 *Llanthony Abbey* built 1/23, withdrawn 11/38 (rebuilt). E148 No. 6918, E95, D95, E127+, –.

161. No. 4042 *Prince Albert* built 5/13, withdrawn 11/51. D94, C54, E127, H8/11, E85+, D94, E79, F13, F13.

162. No. 2913 *Saint Andrew* built 8/07, withdrawn 5/48. C32, D30, SR (ex-LSWR) Ironclads, C–, –.

163. No. 4028 *Roumanian Monarch* built 9/09, withdrawn 1/52. D56, C59, C62, H32-H31-H30, E88, E127+, D95.

164. No. 4055 *Princess Sophia* built 7/14, withdrawn 2/51, –.

165. No. 5934 *Kneller Hall* built 6/33, withdrawn 5/64. E95, LMS, LMS, –.

166. No. 2869 built 10/18, withdrawn 6/59.

167. No. 5030 *Shireburn Castle* built 5/34, withdrawn 9/62. E145-E145 'B' set.

168. No. 6009 *King Charles II* built 3/28, withdrawn 9/62. E140-E140 'B' set, –.

169. No. 5506 built 10/27 withdrawn 5/64. E82, C75, C66, C66, C61/3, C66, C66, E147, –.

170. No. 5540 built 7/28, withdrawn 8/60. E145-E145 'B' set.

171. Bristol Temple Meads.

172. Bristol Temple Meads.

173. South end of Bristol Temple Meads Station.

174. Bristol East.

175. No. 5026 *Cricceith Castle* built 4/34, withdrawn 11/64. D124, E151, C73, C54+, D94, E110/112, LNER fish.

176. No. 5005 *Manorbier Castle* built 6/27, withdrawn 2/60. D88, E127+, C31, –.

177. No. 4037 *The South Wales Borderers* built 12/10, rebuilt 6/26, withdrawn 9/62. C54+, D107, –.

178. No. 4081 *Warwick Castle* built 3/24, withdrawn 1/63. E105, C54+, C54+, –.

179. No. 5800 built 1/33, withdrawn 9/62. N15, N8, K40.

180. No. 5019 *Treago Castle* built 7/32, withdrawn 9/62. E82, H38, E128, LMS (ex-LNWR D312), LMS, LMS, D–, E–, –.

181. No. 5011 *Tintagel Castle* built 7/27, withdrawn 9/62. N14, C32, E154/5, –, C17 in siding.

182. No. 2933 *Bibury Court* built 11/11, withdrawn 1/53. C64, E146/8, D117, C59.

183. 'Hall' class. O11, D95, E127+, E127+, C54+, D94.

184. No. 5013 *Abergavenny Castle* built 6/32, withdrawn 7/62. L22, E69+, LMS BSK D1720, LMS, O33, D45+, E85+, D115, –.

185. No. 6003 *King George IV* built 7/27, withdrawn 6/62. D51, C44+, H11, A20, D69, C44+, –.

186. No. 4084 *Aberystwyth Castle* built 5/25, withdrawn 10/60. H54, D94.

187. No. 6015 *King Richard III* built 6/28, withdrawn 9/62. F20, D82/84, E93, D83/90, E128+, H13/14, –, down from back, D106, E137, H8/11, C59, E137, –.

188. No. 4022 *Belgian Monarch* built 6/09, withdrawn 2/52. G20, C74, C17, LMS (ex-MR), –.

189. No. 2933 *Bibury Court* built 11/11, withdrawn 1/53. E83, E128, D–, E79, –.

190. No. 4365 built 7/15, withdrawn 4/48. E140-E140 'B' set, C–, C67.

191. No. 5008 *Raglan Castle* built 6/27, withdrawn 9/62. K40, E127+, H25/33, D43, E102, C27, –, –, –, O33.

192. No. 5048 *Cranbrook Castle* built 4/36, withdrawn 8/62. D108, E115/8, H8/11, E127+, C59, D95, –.

193. No. 2955 *Tortworth Court* built 4/13, withdrawn 3/50. K30, C62, E118, E73, H15, D115, C54.

194. No. 2261 built 4/30, withdrawn 9/64. O11, –.

195. No. 5014 *Goodrich Castle* built 6/32, withdrawn 2/65. D95+, E127+, –.

196. No. 6018 *King Henry VI* built 6/28, withdrawn 10/63. –.

197. No. 2940 *Dorney Court* built 12/11, withdrawn 1/52. D51, E93, D51/57, C29, D43, –.

198. No. 4064 *Reading Abbey* built 12/22, withdrawn 2/37 (rebuilt).

199. No. 1163 built 3/76, withdrawn 5/46.

200. No. 1008 built 1899 M&SWJ Rly. No. 28. Rebuilt by the GWR 3/27, withdrawn 12/36.

201. No. 2928 *Saint Sebastian* built 9/07, withdrawn 8/48. C10, E140-E140 'B' set.

202. No. 4119 built 11/36, withdrawn 9/63. C67, C62, D25+, A7, C16, D25+, O4.

203. No. 504- Castle class. D121, C73, A20, H41, E154, –.

204. No. 4033 *Queen Victoria* built 11/10, withdrawn 6/51. D104, C70, C70, H32-H31-H30, A13, C70, D–.

205. No. 5012 *Berry Pomeroy Castle* built 7/27, withdrawn 4/62. E80, C33, E98, H19, C54+, D83/90, D82/84, E109/111, –, foreground, SR (ex-LSWR) 30' PBV, LNER CCT, LNER CCT, Horseboxes.

206. No. 4941 *Llangedwyn Hall* built 7/29, withdrawn 10/62. LNER van No. 505303.

207. No. 5940 *Whitbourne Hall* built 8/33, withdrawn 9/62. LNER van, LNER van, C10, E82.
208. No. 7207 built 10/34, withdrawn 11/64. SR 8plank, V–, SC No. 5512, –.
209. No. 4015 *Knight of St. John* built 3/08, withdrawn 2/51. D108, C73, C73, H32-H31-H30, E127+, E127+, D95.
210. No. 4079 *Pendennis Castle* built 2/24, withdrawn 5/64 (preserved). E114, C33, C32, C32, C67, –.
211. No. 5000 *Launceston Castle* built 9/26, withdrawn 10/64. E114, D56, E132, D95, C58, H25/33, E69+, –.
212. No. 4908 *Broome Hall* built 1/29, withdrawn 10/63. D70, C67, C30, E127+, E88, LMS, LMS, C17, C32, D103.
213. No. 5039 *Rhuddlan Castle* built 6/35, withdrawn 6/64. D121, C70, E151, H11, C27, D121, E151, D121, –.
214. No. 5566 built 1/29, withdrawn 1/59. C10, F14, C14, C3, C10, C10, C22, E–, –.
215. No. 9311 built 3/32, withdrawn 10/63. LMS, Wm. Perch, Rigus, –, O–, J–, J–, –.
216. No. 2940 *Dorney Court* built 12/11, withdrawn 1/52. C10, E116-E116 'B' set, O11, O11, LNER van.
217. No. 4019 *Knight Templar* built 5/08, withdrawn 10/49. D104, C70, C70, H32-H31-H30, A13, C70, D–.
218. No. 4096 *Highclere Castle* built 6/26, withdrawn 1/63. K15, D52, E66+, H38, D118, E127+, D94.
219. No. 4046 *Princess Mary* built 5/14, withdrawn 11/51. N16, LMS, E148, E98, D95, LMS diner, –.
220. No. 3363 *Alfred Baldwin* built 1/03, withdrawn 10/49. F10, C23.
221. No. 6805 *Broughton Grange* built 9/36, withdrawn 3/61. G20, C32, D70, E69+, D30/31, C44+, C44+, –.
222. No. 5012 *Berry Pomeroy Castle* built 7/27, withdrawn 4/62. C44+, E152, H26+, D–, C–, C–, D121, E151, C70, D121.
223. No. 6811 *Cranbourne Grange* built 11/36, withdrawn 7/64. G20, C31, D116, E143, C54+, D115, E88.
224. No. 4949 *Packwood Hall* built 8/29, withdrawn 9/64. K26/9, D127, E154, LMS diner D1857, LMS BTK, LMS CK, LMS BTK, –.
225. No. 4031 *Queen Mary* built 10/10, withdrawn 6/51. LMS stock –.
226. No. 2820 built 12/05, withdrawn 11/58.
227. No. 6343 built 3/23, withdrawn 9/60. LNER 5 plank, LMS 5 plank, –.
228. No. 3356 *Sir Stafford* built 11/00, withdrawn 1/36. AAC Anthracite, Evans & Bevan, O–, –, LMS, –.
229. No. 4261 built 5/17, withdrawn 3/59. LNER 5 plank.
230. No. 5771 built 9/29, withdrawn 3/61. V23, LNER (ex-GE) van, Sully & Co., Baldwin, Sully & Co., –.
231. No. 3031 built 1917, withdrawn 5/56. N6 No. 33062, N4 No. 53160, N2, N2, –.
232. Ashton Gate swing bridge.
233. No. 4060 *Princess Eugenie* built 7/14, withdrawn 10/52. E69+, C30+, –, E127+, –.
234. No. 2915 *Saint Bartholomew* built 8/07, withdrawn 10/50. C62, C4, C10, –.
235. D.R.C. No. 15 built 4/36, withdrawn 1/59.
236. D.R.C. No. 8 built 3/36, withdrawn 1/59.
237. No. 5806 built 1/33, withdrawn 6/57.
238. No. 8307 built 1/17, withdrawn 11/56. W8, Mink A, Mink A, Mink A, Mink A, Mica, Mica, Mica, Mica, Mica, Mink A, –.
239. No. 502- 'Castle' class. C27, C62, C62, E66+, H8/11, D56, C62, C70, E148, C67, E–.
240. No. 6014 *King Henry VII* built 5/28, withdrawn 9/62. M10, H46, G60, H45, H40, H39, E109/11, C44+, D82/84.
241. No. 6023 *King Edward II* built 6/30, withdrawn 6/62. D105, E137, H39, H40, E137, C59, D105, E148.
242. No. 6009 *King Charles II* built 3/28, withdrawn 9/62. D56, –.
243. No. 4064 *Reading Abbet* built 12/22, withdrawn 2/37 (rebuilt) E95, E128, D43, E109/11, D43, –.
244. 43XX C10, C23, C58, C30+, SR, SR, SR, SR, C54+.
245. No. 6007 *King William III* built 3/28, withdrawn 9/62. D120, C69, H44, H43, –.

246. No. 6025 *King Henry III* built 7/30, withdrawn 12/62. D43, C44+, E109/111, D83/90, H8/11, –.
247. No. 4077 *Chepstow Castle* built 2/24, withdrawn 8/62. D43, C44+, E–, –.
248. No. 4595 built 4/27, withdrawn 12/58, No. 5549 built 10/28, withdrawn 1/62. SR stock, set No. 326?
249. No. 4076 *Carmarthen Castle* built 2/24, withdrawn 2/63. D43, C27, E109/11, H8/11, D43, E–, D43, –.
250. No. 6000 *King George V* built 6/27, withdrawn 12/62 (preserved). D120, E149, C69, C32+, C54+, D–, H8/11, –.
251. No. 6025 *King Henry III* built 7/30, withdrawn 12/62. C54+, C62, C62, C62, C44+ C29, C27, D127, E158, E158, –, H52, C73, C–.
252. No. 6018 *King Henry VI* built 6/28, withdrawn 12/62. D121, C70, E155, H40, H39, E158, E158, D127, C–, C–, –.
253. No. 6028 *King George VI* built 7/30, withdrawn 11/62. D118, C73, E154/5, –.
254. No. 6014 *King Henry VII* built 5/28, withdrawn 9/62. E150, E150, D120, E149, –.
255. No. 2927 *Saint Patrick* built 9/07, withdrawn 12/51. D95, C24, C29, C17, H15/19, –.
256. No. 6023 *King Edward II* built 6/30, withdrawn 6/62.
257. No. 6009 *King Charles II* built 3/28, withdrawn 9/62. D83+, E110/112, D43, C24, –.
258. No. 6028 *King George VI* built 7/30, withdrawn 11/62. D47, C29, C44+, C24, C27, C44+, E–, –.
259. No. 4085 *Berkeley Castle* built 5/25, withdrawn 5/60. K41, D43, H16, C29, E103, D43.
260. No. 5022 *Wigmore Castle* built 8/32, withdrawn 12/63. E82, H41, D56, C32, C29/33, D45+.
261. No. 4074 *Caldicot Castle* built 12/23, withdrawn 10/63. D45, E127, C54, E137, C70, D94, H15, –.
262. No. 5043 *Barbury Castle* built 3/36, withdrawn 12/63 (preserved). D104, C62, E127+, E127+, D116, C67, H13/14, E128.
263. No. 6014 *King Henry VI* built 5/28, withdrawn 9/62. D121, C70, E154, H41, –.
264. No. 5344 built 3/18, withdrawn 9/58. –.
265. No. 4969 *Shrugborough Hall* built 12/29, withdrawn 9/62. V–, LMS van, O8, J–, –.
266. No. 5910 *Park Hall* built 6/31, withdrawn 9/62. V–, V–, V–, V–, –.
267. Interior of Filton Incline Signal Box.
268. No. 4999 *Gopsal Hall* built 3/31, withdrawn 9/62. LMS (ex-LNWR, D436) horsebox, E114, E128, E127+, H38, D45+, E127+, D95, D94, C–, –.
269. No. 5004 *Llanstephan Castle* built 6/27, withdrawn 4/62. H17/18, H13/14, E139, D107, E79, D107, D43, E104, M10.
270. 315X, 28CC class. –.
271. No. 5008 *Raglan Castle* built 6/27, withdrawn 9/62. E82, LMS BTK (ex-LNWR, D313A), LMS CK(ex-LNWR, D131), LMS BTK (ex-LNWR, D306), LMS diner D1811, C54+, E154/5, –.
272. No. 6016 *King Edward V* built 6/28, withdrawn 11/63. L22, C24, –.
273. No. 2675 built 11/02, withdrawn 9/35. –.
274. No. 3446 *Goldfinch* built 11/09, withdrawn 12/48. O22+, D95, C54+, E127+, –.
275. 315X, 28XX class. –.
276. No. 5260 built 3/26, withdrawn –/35. (rebuilt) LMS, LMS, tar tank, Baldwin, Baldwin, LMS (ex-MR), –.
277. 53XX class. D56/80, C54+, A18, C49, –.
278. 4575 class. C10, C43, –.
Appen. No. 4093 *Dunster Castle* built 5/26, withdrawn 9/64. C24, E113, H15, E114, D95, –.

Bibliography

In addition to the books listed previously, students and enthusiasts will find the following works of particular interest.

RCTS Locos of the GWR, part 13. – RCTS.
GW Diesel Railcars (& Supplement) – Russell – Wild Swan.
Rail Centres, Bristol – Maggs – Ian Allan.
GW Travelling Post Offices – Hosegood – Wild Swan.
GW Coaches Appendix, Vols 1 & 2 – Russell – O.P.C.
An Historical Survey of GW Stations, Vols 1 – 4, – Clark and Potts – O.P.C.
GW Company Servants – Russell – Wild Swan.
An Illustrated History of LNWR coaches – Jenkinson – O.P.C.
Midland Railway Carriages – Lacy & Dow – Wild Swan.
A Pictorial Record of GW Architecture – Vaughan – O.P.C.
The GW at Swindon Works – Peck – O.P.C.

Acknowledgements

As always with a work such as this, it would be impossible to complete without the aid and assistance of others. We wish to thank all of those who have written offering support and encouragement. We would like to thank the following especially, for their help and information:- Mrs. M. Soole; the staff of the National Railway Museum; members of the Great Western Study Group, David Cross and Keith Ettle of Bristol, Rev. N. Pocock of Cornwall, Peter Jones of Nuneaton and David Fraser. We must also thank Margaret again for the typing and the encouragement and support of our publisher, Roger Hardingham. Last but by no means least, our long suffering wives, Dorothy and Margery, and families for their great help and patience.